State v. Alexander

Cases and Materials

Professor Charles H. Rose, III

-Notes-

STATE V. ALEXANDER

PROFESSOR CHARLES H. ROSE III

"We empower students to find within themselves their unique voices – to become the best possible advocates they can be."

The ideas behind using case files to teach are grounded in concepts of experiential learning. It is in doing that true education occurs.[1] These files are designed to create optimal "learning by doing" opportunities – the foundation upon which advocacy instruction, if not all learning, rests.

State v. Alexander Case File, 2nd Edition
Broken Tower Press
ISBN: 978-1-7335318-0-1
Copyright Charles H. Rose III, All Rights Reserved,
December 2018

---

[1] Myles Horton, the co-founder of the Highlander Folk School, referred to this with a phrase from a Spanish song that translated reads "We make the road by walking." This is one of the best captured thoughts about experiential learning I have ever read.

CASE FILE CONTENTS

Tab A: Introduction

- Introduction to the Case
- Indictment
- Jury Instructions
- Verdict Form

Tab B: Police Investigations

- Officer Report of Incident – Alexander Murder
- Detective Investigative Report – Alexander Murder
    - Diagram of Alexander Neighborhood. Prepared by ABW
    - Diagram of Alexander home. Prepared by ABW
    - Diagram of Alexander home foyer. Prepared by ABW
    - Letter dated 5/15/20XX-2. Taken from jacket of Chris Alexander
    - Letter dates 6/1/20XX-2. Taken from jacket of Chris Alexander
    - Business Card taken from Chris Alexander's wallet
    - Photo of Wendy's bag of food. Taken by EM
    - Photo of bag found in Wendy's bag in Alexander home. Taken by ABW
    - Photo of baggie found in Wendy's bag in Alexander home. Taken by ABW
    - Photo of .45 pistol. Found in Alexander home by ABW
    - Photo of 9mm pistol. Produced by EM
    - Photo of exterior door of Alexander home. Taken by EM
    - Photo 1 of interior door of Alexander home. Taken by EM
    - Photo 2of interior door of Alexander home. Taken by EM
    - Photo 3 of interior door of Alexander home. Taken by EM
    - Photo 4 of interior door of Alexander home. Taken by EM
    - Photo of slugs removed from door frame by ABW
    - Photo of slugs taken from concrete floor by EM
    - Photo of .45 ammo found in Alexander home. Taken by ABW
    - Photo of skid marks outside of Alexander home. Taken by EM

- - Shooting Club sign in sheet
- Officer Incident Report – Drug Activity

Tab C: Witness Statements
- Statement of Robert Hightower
- Statement of Nikki Long
- Statement of Sharon Barry
- Statement of Doris Presley
- Statement of Billy Bob Schifflett
- 2nd Statement of Nikki Long
- Statement of Anece Baxter-White
- Deposition of Roger Curlin
- Deposition of Dr. Jeremiah Jones
- Testimony of Brandi Alexander

Tab D: Reports & Certificates
- Chris Alexander Death Certificate
- Coroner's Report
- Chain of Custody documents
- Lab Report and Certificate
- PDQ Alarm System Report
- Cell Phone Record Report

Tab E: News Coverage
- Pelican Bay Star, Nov. 3, 20XX-2 "Doctor Horrible"
- Pelican Bay Star, Dec. 7, 20XX-2 "DA Argues Infidelity, Money Motivated Killing"
- Pelican Bay Star, Dec. 9, 20XX-2 "Detective: Suspect Lied Night of Husband's Death"
- Pelican Bay Star, Dec. 13, 20XX-2 "Teacher's Attorney Blasts Investigation: Defense Claims Detective Left Details Out of Report"

- Pelican Bay Star, Jan. 1, 20XX-1 "Teacher's Murder Trial Resumes"
- Pelican Bay Star, Jan. 4, 20XX-1 "Juror Dismissed in Ex-Teacher's Murder Trial"
- Pelican Bay Star, Jan. 9, 20XX-1 "Teacher Guilty!"
- Pelican Bay Star, Nov. 15, 20XX-1 "Retrial Set For Teacher Charged with Murder"

Tab F: Conviction Reports

- Chris Alexander Drug Conviction Record
- Nikki Long Filing False Police Report Conviction Record
- Nikki Long Possession Conviction Record

**IN THE CIRCUIT COURT OF THE FIRST JUDICIAL DISTRICT OF
CALUSA COUNTY, XXXXX**

STATE OF XXXXX,
v.

BRANDI ALEXANDER,

Defendant.   CASE NO.: 0318-20XX

INDICTMENT

I.   MURDER FIRST DEGREE

IN THE NAME AND BY THE AUTHORITY OF THE STATE OF XXXXX:
The Grand Jurors of the State of XXXXX, duly called, impaneled, and sworn to inquire and true presentment make, in and for the body of the County of Calusa, upon their oaths, present that on or about the 6th day of June, 20XX-2, within the County of Calusa, State of XXXXX, BRANDI ALEXANDER did unlawfully from a premeditated design to effect the death of a human being, kill and murder CHRISTOPHER ALEXANDER, a human being, by shooting him multiple times with a firearm, in violation of XXXXX Statute 118.01, to the evil example of all others in like cases offending and against the peace and dignity of the State of XXXXX.

A TRUE BILL:

George Peabody Smalley
Foreperson of the Grand Jury

I, Prosecutor for the Circuit Court in the First Judicial District, in and for Calusa County, XXXXX, do hereby aver, as authorized and required by law, that I have acted in an advisory capacity to the Grand Jurors of Calusa County previous to their returning the above indictment in the above-styled case.

Nick Cox

PROSECUTOR
FIRST JUDICIAL DISTRICT
CALUSA COUNTY

Presented before: the Honorable Jeanne Jordan, 1st Judicial Circuit, Calusa County, XXXXX

JURY INSTRUCTION NO.: 1

Plea of Not Guilty; Reasonable Doubt; and Burden of Proof

The defendant has entered a plea of not guilty. This means you must presume or believe the defendant is innocent. The presumption stays with the defendant as to each material allegation in the [information] [indictment] through each stage of the trial unless it has been overcome by the evidence to the exclusion of and beyond a reasonable doubt.

To overcome the defendant's presumption of innocence, the State has the burden of proving the crime with which the defendant is charged was committed and the defendant is the person who committed the crime.

The defendant is not required to present evidence or prove anything.

Whenever the words "reasonable doubt" are used you must consider the following:

A reasonable doubt is not a mere possible doubt, a speculative, imaginary or forced doubt. Such a doubt must not influence you to return a verdict of not guilty if you have an abiding conviction of guilt. On the other hand, if, after carefully considering, comparing and weighing all the evidence, there is not an abiding conviction of guilt, or, if, having a conviction, it is one which is not stable but one which wavers and vacillates, then the charge is not proved beyond every reasonable doubt and you must find the defendant not guilty because the doubt is reasonable.

It is to the evidence introduced in this trial, and to it alone, that you are to look for that proof.

A reasonable doubt as to the guilt of the defendant may arise from the evidence, conflict in the evidence, or the lack of evidence.

If you have a reasonable doubt, you should find the defendant not guilty. If you have no reasonable doubt, you should find the defendant guilty.

JURY INSTRUCTION NO.: 2

Murder — First Degree
§ 782.04(1)(A), Stat.

To prove the crime of First Degree Premeditated Murder, the State must prove the following three elements beyond a reasonable doubt:

1.   (Victim) is dead.

2.   The death was caused by the criminal act of (defendant).

3.   There was a premeditated killing of (victim).

An "act" includes a series of related actions arising from and performed pursuant to a single design or purpose.

"Killing with premeditation" is killing after consciously deciding to do so. The decision must be present in the mind at the time of the killing. The law does not fix the exact period of time that must pass between the formation of the premeditated intent to kill and the killing. The period of time must be long enough to allow reflection by the defendant. The premeditated intent to kill must be formed before the killing.

The question of premeditation is a question of fact to be determined by you from the evidence. It will be sufficient proof of premeditation if the circumstances of the killing and the conduct of the accused convince you beyond a reasonable doubt of the existence of premeditation at the time of the killing.

JURY INSTRUCTION NO.: 3

Murder — Second Degree
§ 782.04(2), Stat.

To prove the crime of Second Degree Murder, the State must prove the following three elements beyond a reasonable doubt:

1.   (Victim) is dead.

2.   The death was caused by the criminal act of (defendant).

3.   There was an unlawful killing of (victim) by an act imminently dangerous to another and demonstrating a depraved mind without regard for human life.

An "act" includes a series of related actions arising from and performed pursuant to a single design or purpose.

An act is "imminently dangerous to another and demonstrating a depraved mind" if it is an act or series of acts that:

1.   a person of ordinary judgment would know is reasonably certain to kill or do serious bodily injury to another, and

2.   is done from ill will, hatred, spite, or an evil intent, and

3.   is of such a nature that the act itself indicates an indifference to human life.

In order to convict of Second Degree Murder, it is not necessary for the State to prove the defendant had an intent to cause death.

JURY INSTRUCTION NO.: 4

Weighing the Evidence

It is up to you to decide what evidence is reliable. You should use your common sense in deciding which is the best evidence, and which evidence should not be relied upon in considering your verdict. You may find some of the evidence not reliable, or less reliable than other evidence.

You should consider how the witnesses acted, as well as what they said. Some things you should consider are:

1.   Did the witness seem to have an opportunity to see and know the things about which the witness testified?

2.   Did the witness seem to have an accurate memory?

3.   Was the witness honest and straightforward in answering the attorneys' questions?

4.   Did the witness have some interest in how the case should be decided?

5.   Does the witness's testimony agree with the other testimony and other evidence in the case?

JURY INSTRUCTION NO.: 5

Rules for Deliberation

These are some general rules that apply to your discussion. You must follow these rules in order to return a lawful verdict:

1.   You must follow the law as it is set out in these instructions. If you fail to follow the law, your verdict will be a miscarriage of justice. There is no reason for failing to follow the law in this case. All of us are depending upon you to make a wise and legal decision in this matter.

2.   This case must be decided only upon the evidence that you have heard from the testimony of the witnesses [and have seen in the form of the exhibits in evidence] and these instructions.

3.   This case must not be decided for or against anyone because you feel sorry for anyone, or are angry at anyone.

4.   Remember, the lawyers are not on trial. Your feelings about them should not influence your decision in this case.

5.   Your verdict should not be influenced by feelings of prejudice, bias, or sympathy. Your verdict must be based on the evidence, and on the law contained in these instructions.

In closing, let me remind you that it is important that you follow the law spelled out in these instructions in deciding your verdict. There are no other laws that apply to this case. Even if you do not like the laws that must be applied, you must use them. For two centuries we have lived by the constitution and the law. No juror has the right to violate rules we all share.

IN THE CIRCUIT COURT OF TWENTIETH JUDICIAL DISTRICT
CALUSA COUNTY, XXXXX
CRIMINAL DIVISION
VERDICT FORM

State   )
)
) CASE NO.: 20XX-**2-183**
)
v.   ) DIVISION:
)
)
Alexander.   )
)

We, the Jury, return the following verdict, and each of us concerns in this verdict:

(Choose the appropriate verdict)

I.   NOT GUILTY

We, the jury, find the defendant, Christopher Alexander, NOT GUILTY.

_____
Foreperson

II.   FIRST DEGREE MURDER

To prove the crime of First Degree Premeditated Murder, the State must prove the following three elements beyond a reasonable doubt:

1.   (Victim) is dead.

2.   The death was caused by the criminal act of (defendant).

3.   There was a premeditated killing of (victim).

We, the jury, find the defendant, Christopher Alexander, GUILTY of Murder in the First Degree.

_____
Foreperson

III. SECOND DEGREE MURDER

To prove the crime of Second Degree Murder, the State must prove the following three elements beyond a reasonable doubt:

1. (Victim) is dead.

2. The death was caused by the criminal act of (defendant).

3. There was an unlawful killing of (victim) by an act imminently dangerous to another and demonstrating a depraved mind without regard for human life.

We, the jury, find the defendant, Christopher Alexander, GUILTY of Murder in the Second Degree.

_____
Foreperson

CALUSA POLICE DEPARTMENT
CALUSA COUNTY

INCIDENT REPORT

OFFICER'S NAME:	DATE:		TIME:	LOCATION:
A B-White	6-6-20XX-2		2301 hours	West Calusa Hills

COMPLAINANT'S NAME:		DOB:	ADDRESS:	CITY / STATE ZIP
PDQ Alarm Systems			6731 Lullaby Lane	Pelican Bay, XX 33707

HOME PHONE NUMBER:	WORK PHONE NUMBER:	MOBILE/PAGER NUMBER:
		n/a

ALLEGED SUSPECT'S NAME:		DOB:	ADDRESS:	CITY / STATE ZIP
Brandi Alexander			6731 Lullaby Lane	Pelican Bay, XX 33707

HOME PHONE NUMBER:	WORK PHONE NUMBER:	MOBILE/PAGER NUMBER:
555-5172	555-6382	555-3327

(W1) WITNESS'S NAME:	DOB:	ADDRESS:	CITY / STATE ZIP
Doris Presley	2-4-51	Lullaby Lane	Pelican Bay, XX 33707

HOME PHONE NUMBER:	WORK PHONE NUMBER:	MOBILE/PAGER NUMBER:

(W2) WITNESS'S NAME:	DOB:	ADDRESS:	CITY / STATE ZIP
Robert Hightower	10/31-64	Lullaby lance	Pelican Bay, XX 33707

HOME PHONE NUMBER:	WORK PHONE NUMBER:	MOBILE/PAGER NUMBER:
555-8442	555-0997	555-3997

WRITE COMPLETE DETAILED REPORT:

The department received a call at the station from an alarm service that was reporting a shooting at a home on Lullaby lane. I proceeded directly to the home, arriving in approximately 10 minutes. Upon arrival I observed that the front door was open with light on inside the home. Neighbors were gathered at the homes on both sides of the house in question, as well as in the front yards across the street. Upon approaching the house I noticed the smell of burning rubber and noted that there were skid marks that appeared to be fresh in front of the home on Lullaby lane, on the road itself.

OFFICER'S SIGNATURE	PRINTED NAME / RANK / BADGE NUMBER
Anece Baxter-White	Anece Baxter-White Patrolman #4613

Lights were on in the home and the front door appeared open. I proceeded to the front door, identifying myself as a police officer. Upon arriving in the home I noticed shell casings on the ground outside and inside the front door. A woman was weeping uncontrollably while kneeling next to the body of a man — she appeared to be trying to wake him up.

I inspected the body laying in the foyer. It was clear that several shots had been fired into the body, specifically two shots or more to the groin. I noticed that there were several bullet holes in the floor underneath the body, and I found at least one bullet lodged in the door frame of the foyer. I also found two notes that are attached to this incident report in the pocket of the dead man, as well as a business card in his wallet.

Looking around the house I noted that the television was on very loud in the den next to the foyer. Upon entering the den I noted the presence of a Wendy's food bag. Inside the bag was a cheeseburger and fries. Underneath the cheeseburger I found 1 plastic bag of what appeared to be marijuana and an additional small bag of white powder. I conducted field tests and results indicated that the powder contained cocaine and the green leafy substance was marijuana. After speaking with the wife it was determined that a GSR test of her hands was not necessary. My team and I left after questioning the wife.

Upon arriving at the station instructed to return to the Alexander home to assist in additional investigation.

OFFICER'S SIGNATURE	PRINTED NAME / RANK / BADGE NUMBER
Anece Baxter-White	Anece Baxter—White/officer/#4613

INITIALS
ABW

Returned to the home. Retrieved 6 remnants of slugs, 2 from the door jamb and 4 from the floor. Retrieved box of .45 caliber ammunition provided by Ms. Alexander. All evidence gathered was taken to the evidence room. Photos were forward to detective Edwin Morris, along with diagrams of the area.

Investigations continues.

OFFICER'S SIGNATURE	PRINTED NAME / RANK / BADGE NUMBER		
Anece Baxter-White	Anece Baxter—White/officer/#4613		

REPORTING OFFICER	Anece Baxter-White	DATE REPORTED	6/6/20XX-2
REPORTING OFFICER	*Anece Baxter-White*	#4613	6/7/20XX-2
	SIGNATURE	OFFICER BADGE	DATE
REVIEWING SUPERVISOR	*Willie Hightower*	#1240	6/7/20XX-2
	SIGNATURE	OFFICER BADGE	DATE

CALUSA POLICE DEPARTMENT
CALUSA COUNTY

REPORT OF INVESTIGATION
PAGE 1 OF 2

Report No.	Date:	Complaining Witness:
20XX-206060321	6/8/20XX-02	PDQ Alarm Systems

Investigating Officer:	Suspect:
Detective Edwin Morris	Brandi Alexander (wife of decedent)

Division:	Address:
Homicide	6731 Lullabye Lane, Pelican Bay, XX 33707

Victim(s):	Age:	General Description:
Christopher Alexander	32	Male, 72", 195 lbs, Tattoo - Frostie

Investigator's Notes, June 8, 20XX-2:
Case assigned to Homicide division. Opened case file, began investigation.

On June 6, 20XX:-2 Officer Baxter-White and Chief Willie Hightower responded to a PDQ alarm system 911 call indicating an attack at the Alexander residence. Canvassed neighborhood for witnesses. Identified potential individuals to interview. She Prepared diagrams of neighborhood (exhibit 1), Alexander home (exhibit 2), and Interior of Alexander home (exhibit 3). Officer Baxter-White collected two letters from the coat pocket of the deceased (exhibit 4 &5), and a business card from the deceased's wallet (exhibit 6).

June 7, 20XX-2.
Developed diagrams of the relevant areas of Lullaby Lane (exhibit 1,2 and 3 of this report)
Catalogued & Photographed the following evidence seized from the Alexander Home:

- Bag of Wendy's food (exhibit 7)
- Bag of green leafy substance (probable marijuana)(exhibit 8)
- Bag of white powder (probable cocaine) (exhibit 9)
- Photograph of a .45 pistol (note this is a photograph found in the home on the writing desk of Ms. Alexander) (exhibit 10)
- Photograph of a 9mm pistol matching description of that owned by Chris Alexander (exhibit 11)
- Photographs of the bullet holes in the home(exhibits 12, 13, 14, 15, 16)
- Photographs of slugs and ammunition retrieved from Alexander home (exhibits 17, 18, 19)
- Photograph of tire marks on Lullaby Lane(exhibit 20)

June 18, 20XX-2.
Received Coroner's Report, inserted into case file

June 23, 20XX-2.
Visited "From My Cold Dead Hands" Gun Club. Retrieved Sign In Roster for May 25, 20XX-2 and inserted into case file.

July 4, 20XX-2.
Statement of Robert Hightower taken by Edwin Morris

July 8, 20XX-2
Statement of Ms. Nikki Long taken by Edwin Morris

August 12, 20XX-2.
Statement of Ms. Sharon Barry taken. Inserted into case file.
Received statement of Ms. Doris Presley taken by Investigator Stubbs. Inserted into case file.

August 14, 20XX-2.
Received statement of Billy Bob Schifflet taken by Investigator Stubbs. Inserted into case file.

August 15, 20XX-2
Received death certificate from coroner's office, inserted into file

September 23, 20XX-2
Inserted photo of 9mm pistol matching the description of the one owned by Chris Alexander (based upon the firearm registration records for said firearm)

October 10, 20XX-2.
Received results of drug testing. Inserted Lab report and chain of custody document into the file.

October 14, 20XX-2.
Recovered PDQ Alarm Report for month of June 20XX-2. Inserted into case file

Subsequent investigation revealed that Brandi Alexander shot and killed her husband, Chris Alexander, using a .45 caliber weapon. Investigative efforts included interviewing all identified witnesses, recovered evidence and searching for potential weapons registered to the Alexander's. Two weapons were registered to Chris Alexander, a .45 caliber pistol and a 9mm Beretta. I recovered a picture of the .45 registered to Chris Alexander. This picture was provided by Ms. Alexander in accordance with my request. Neither weapon was recovered at the scene. Through proper investigative steps I was able to ascertain that Ms. Alexander was familiar with the .45 caliber weapon, having fired it at the gun range approximately one week prior to the murder. Probable cause clearly exists Brandi Alexander murdered Chris Alexander. Forwarded contents of case file to state prosecutor on October 15, 20XX-2.

Investigation continues.
July 13, 20XX-1. Received affidavit of Officer Anece Baxter-White.
July 19, 20XX-1. Statement of Nikki Long taken by Edwin Morris at Ms. Long's request.

Investigation continues.

Sworn and subscribed in my presence, June 12, 2005. Signature: *Edwin Morris*	I swear and affirm that the report above and the attached files are true and correct to the best of my Belief and Knowledge.
Supervisor: Robert Burrell Supervisor's Signature *Robert Burrell*	Signature: *Edwin Morris*

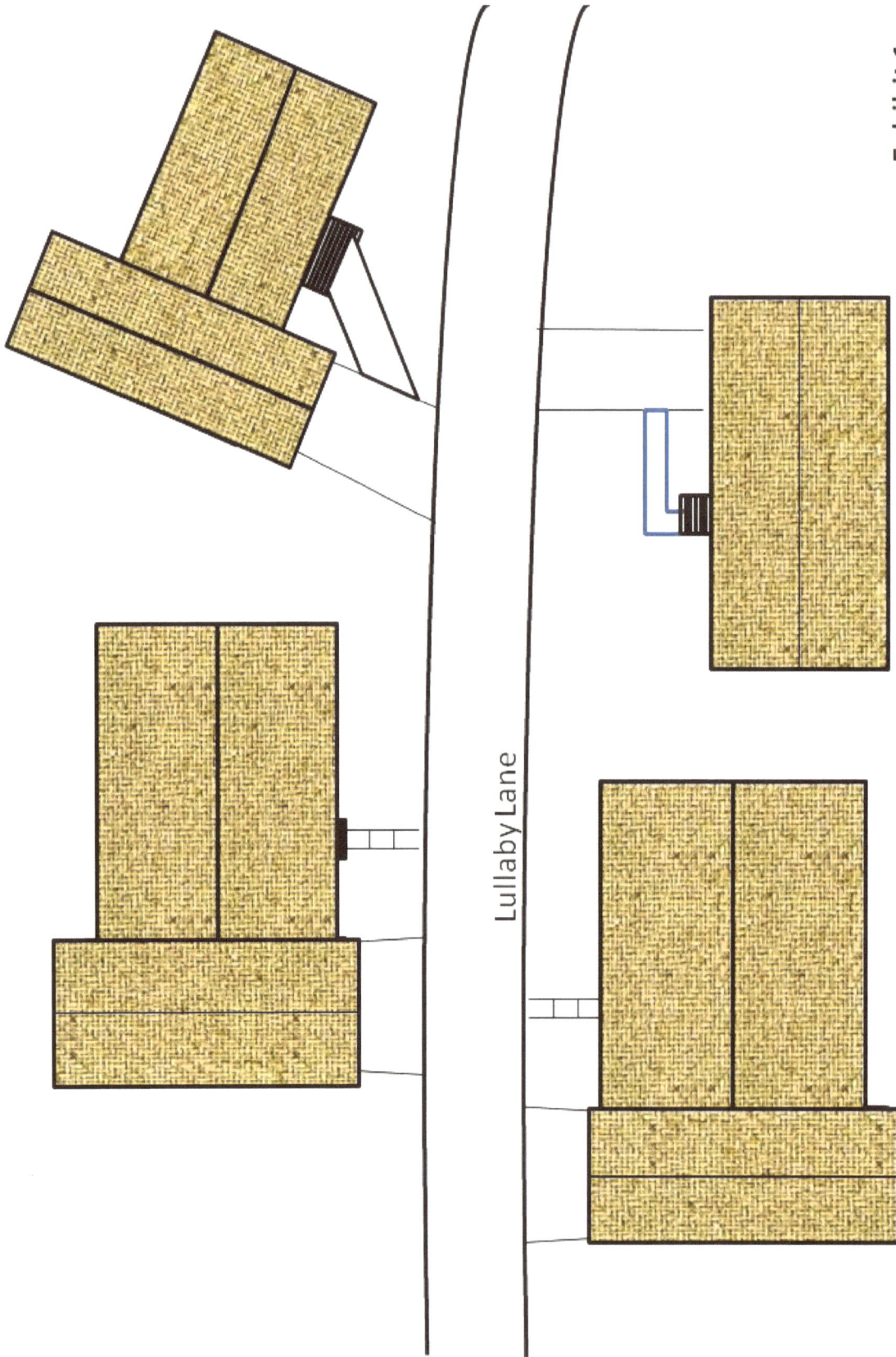

Lullaby Lane

Exhibit 1

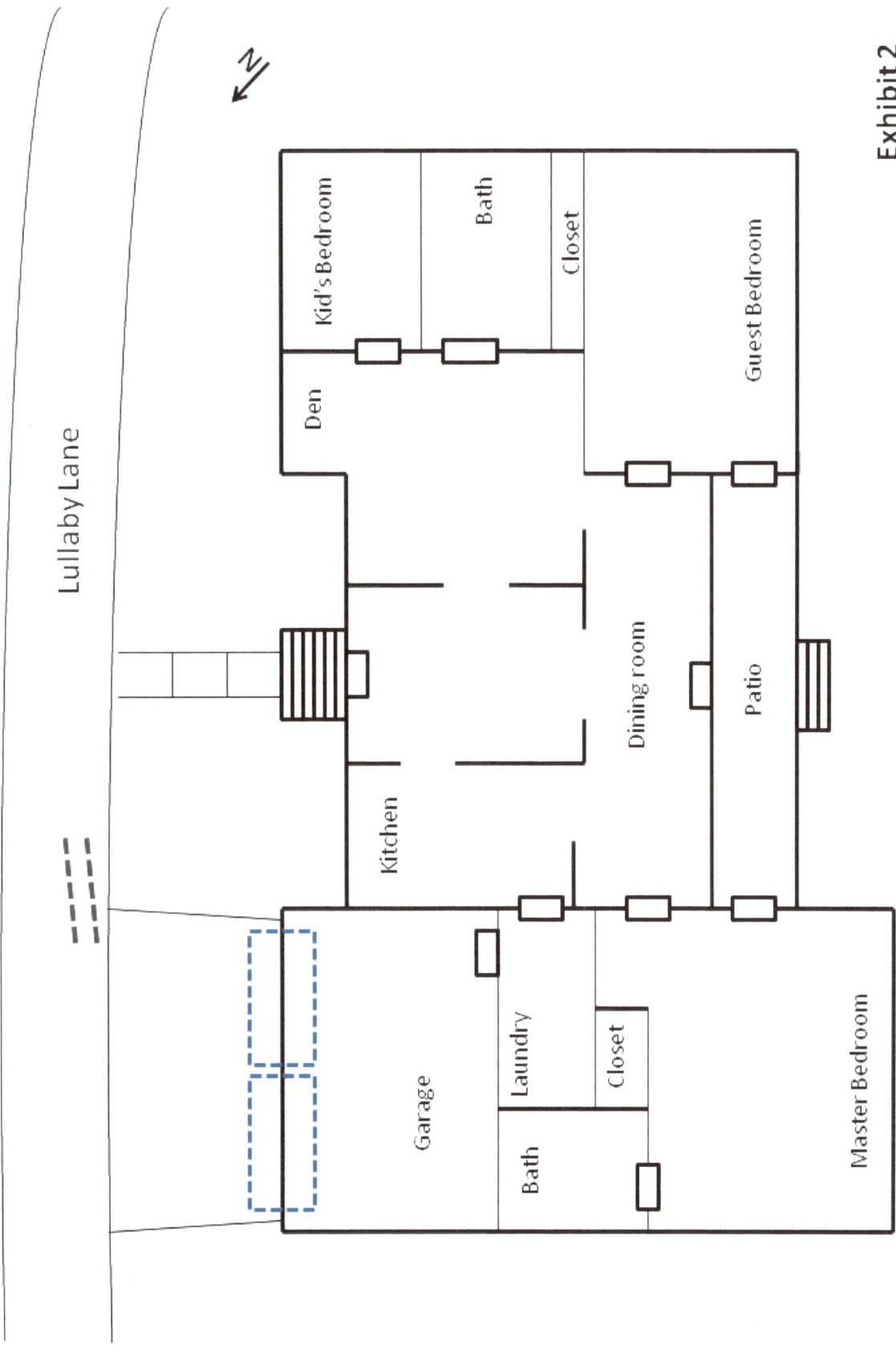

Lullaby Lane

N

Den

Kid's Bedroom

Bath

Closet

Guest Bedroom

Kitchen

Dining room

Patio

Garage

Laundry

Bath

Closet

Master Bedroom

Exhibit 2

State v. Alexander

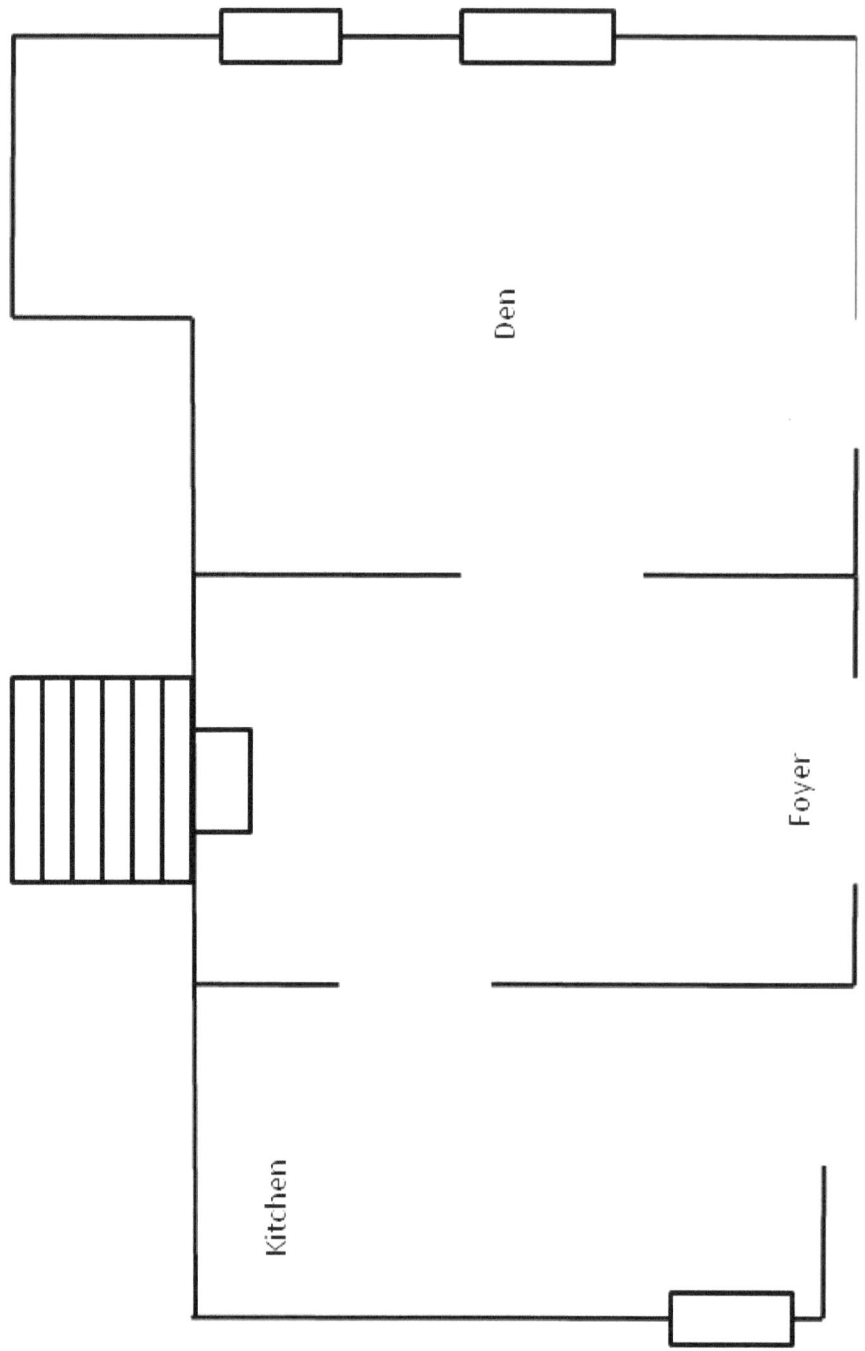

N

Den

Foyer

Kitchen

Exhibit 3

Exhibit 4

Hey Baby!

I was thinking of you tonight and my mind was wandering to when we will finally be together.

That wife of yours is such a bitch! I cannot wait to see her get hers. I will so make you happy. See you tonight!

XL
5/15/20XX-2
XXOOXXOO

Exhibit 5

Babe!

I wish I could see you some mo.

It has been too long since we been together. I'm startin' to think you might not be leaving her — better not be so.

I love you so much and I want us to have a baby together. Please kick that ho to the curb!

TL
6/1/20XX2
Call ME or else . . . .

Exhibit 6

Exhibit 7

Exhibit 8

Exhibit 9

Exhibit 10

Exhibit 11

Exhibit 12

Exhibit 13

Exhibit 14

Exhibit 15

Exhibit 16

Exhibit 17

2 slugs retrieved from door jamb of Alexander home by ABW.
Unable to conduct ballistics testing without a potential
murder weapon.

Edwin Morris   Jun 7, 20XX-2

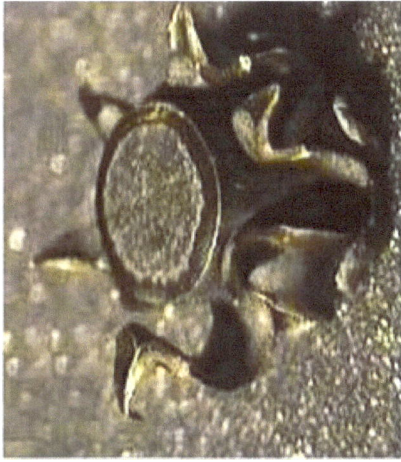

4 slugs I retrieved from concrete floor of Alexander home. Unable to conduct testing without a potential murder weapon, but do match type of ammunition seized from the home..

Edwin Morris   Jun 7, 20XX-2

Exhibit 18

Exhibit 19

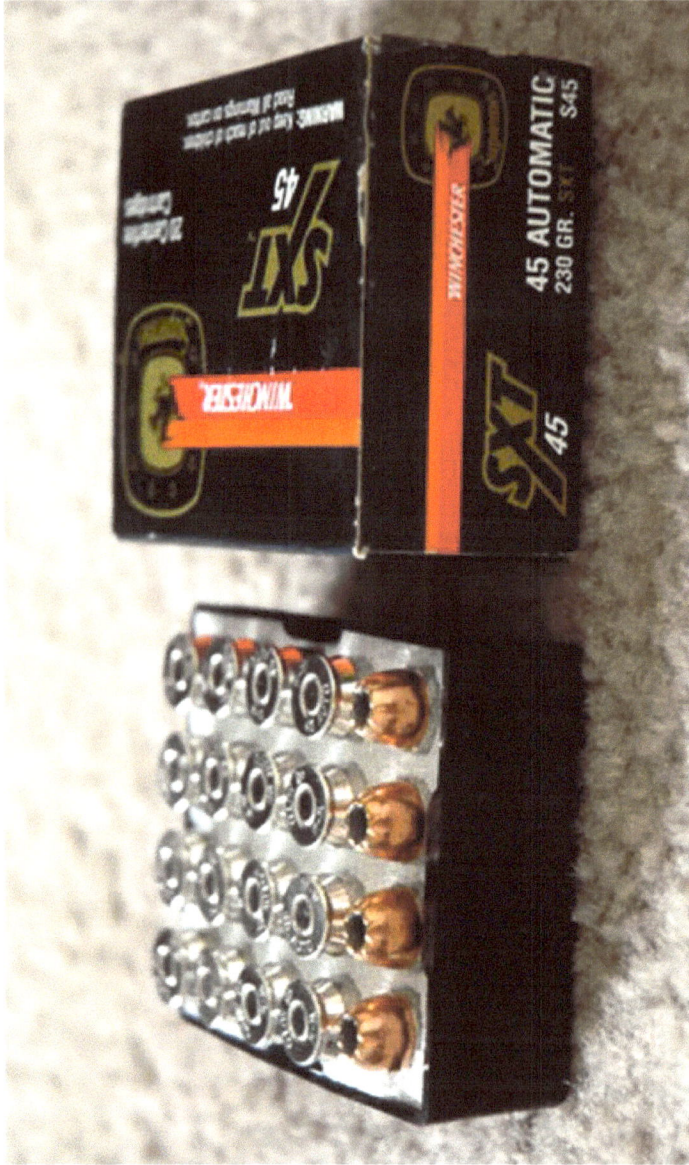

.45 caliber rounds retrieved by ABW from Alexander home on June 6, 20XX-2.

Edwin Morris   Jun 7, 20XX-2

Exhibit 20

From My Cold Dead Hands
Pelican Bay Shooting Club
Sign In Roster

Name (Print & Sign)	Date/Time	Weapon	Range
Donald Sutherland	May 25, 20XX-2 0900 hours	9 MM Glock	2
Tyler Harder	May 25, 20XX-2 0945 hours	.22 caliber rifle	1
Wild Bill Ossmann	May 25, 20XX-2 10:13 AM	MI Carbine	1
Brandi Alexander	May 25, 20XX-2	.45 Pistol	3
Chris Alexander	May 25, 20XX-2 11:25 AM	9 mm	4
Wild Bill Ossmann	May 25, 20XX-2 11:45 AM	.38	4
Norm Pearson	May 25, 20XX-2 1145 hours	.22 target pistol	3
Range closed for maintenance.	1400 hours	B.B.S.	

CALUSA POLICE DEPARTMENT
CALUSA COUNTY

INCIDENT REPORT
PAGE 1 OF 3

OFFICER'S NAME:	DATE:		TIME:		LOCATION:
Willie Alexander	1-6-200x-2		1442		West Calusa Hills

COMPLAINANT'S NAME:		DOB:	ADDRESS:	CITY / STATE ZIP
Robert Hightower			6732 Lullaby Lane	Pelican Bay, XX 33707

HOME PHONE NUMBER:	WORK PHONE NUMBER:	MOBILE/PAGER NUMBER:
727-555-346/	727-555-3465	n/a

ALLEGED SUSPECT'S NAME:	DOB:	ADDRESS:	CITY / STATE ZIP
Alias ~ Frosty	Unknown	Unknown	unknown

HOME PHONE NUMBER:	WORK PHONE NUMBER:	MOBILE/PAGER NUMBER:
n/a	n/a	n/a

(W1) WITNESS'S NAME:		DOB:	ADDRESS:	CITY / STATE ZIP
Juanita Hightower			6732 Lullaby Lane	Pelican Bay, XX 33707

HOME PHONE NUMBER:	WORK PHONE NUMBER:	MOBILE/PAGER NUMBER:

(W2) WITNESS'S NAME:	DOB:	ADDRESS:	CITY / STATE ZIP

Mr. Hightower called the Calusa County Sherrif's Department with a complaint that some unknown guy going by the name of frosty was selling drugs in the neighborhood. He complained that he watched the traffic in the neighborhood and he had noticed a lot of low rider type cars going by his house and parking on the street. Calusa County referred to PBPD.

He also complained because he had called the Pelican Bay police department about gunfire in the neighborhood from some "hoodlums" down the street and nothing had been done. I canvassed the neighborhood but was unable to verify Mr. Hightower's allegations as to Frosty. Will refer to crime stoppers program for additional investigation.

Mr. Hightower appeared combative and irritable when I told him I couldn't fine "Frosty." He muttered something about "taking care of it himself." I smelled incense burning in the Hightower home, but did not observe any improper activity. I did find a group of gang members down the street that I ran off ~ they were just hanging out down the street in front of. I observed no illegal activity.

Investigation Concluded.

OFFICER'S SIGNATURE	PRINTED NAME / RANK / BADGE NUMBER
Alexander	Willie Alexander/SGT/7031D

Report Continued from Page 1:

OFFICER'S SIGNATURE	PRINTED NAME / RANK / BADGE NUMBER
Willie Alexander	Willie Alexander/SGT/7031D

		INITIALS
		WA

REVIEWING SUPERVISOR	Eric Hightower	#1240	1/6/200X-2
	SIGNATURE	OFFICER BADGE	DATE

RH page 1 of 2

My name is Bob Hightower. I am 44 years old. I was born and raised here in Pelican Bay. After high school, I went away to college at the University of Florida, where I received my B.S. in Physics and my Masters degree in Civil Engineering. After college, I decided to move back to Pelican Bay to get a job and start a family. Although I was offered a much higher-paying job in Biloxi, I just couldn't see myself living anywhere other than Pelican Bay. My entire family lives here and I love this city. I've been working at the same civil engineering firm for the past 15 years.

I have two older brothers. My oldest brother, Eric, is the commander of the Pelican Bay Police Department. He was actually the one assigned to investigate Chris Alexander's murder. Well, maybe not the murder itself, but I know he was the one who investigated the crime scene. I love Eric and would do anything for him. I think he is the best cop in the state. He would never lie for any reason and he always does his job perfectly.

My other brother is Ricky. He is the one we do not like to talk about much. You see, he never seemed to care about the consequences of his actions. He was in trouble with the law throughout high school and well into his adult life. Just a few years ago he finally got what was coming to him and was sentenced to twenty-five years for the attempted murder of his live-in girlfriend. He is still in jail and that is where he deserves to stay. He has been nothing but a disgrace to our entire family.

One of the main reasons I don't like Ricky is because he got me caught up in some of his criminal problems a few years back. He approached me around ten years ago to drive him around for work and such because his car broke down. I decided to help him because he had some recent problems with the law and I wanted to help him get his life back in order. Anyway, after I picked him up one day from a friend's house, a police officer pulled me over because I had a broken taillight. My brother told me just to "play it cool." I had no idea what he was talking about. The cop noticed that something was off and asked both of us to step out of the car. They ultimately found marijuana on him and a small bag underneath the seat. Because they were charging me with felony possession, I accepted the prosecutor's plea deal and testified against Ricky. Because I testified, they only gave me six months probation.

The only other legal trouble I had was with the IRS back in the early '90s. It happened because I forgot to include $10,000 worth of investment income on my tax return. The IRS brought charges of fraud and tax evasion against me. However, they eventually dropped the charges because I was very compliant and quickly paid all the taxes, plus penalties, and interest.

RH page 2 of 2

Although I have lived across the street from the Alexanders for several years, I really didn't talk much to either Brandi or Chris. Chris knew my brother, Ricky. So, I guess the adage is true— you know—the company you keep and all. Anyway, I didn't know Brandi or Chris, really. However, I do know a little bit about each of their reputations around town.

With Brandi, I think it is common knowledge that Brandi knew her husband was cheating on her with at least two women. She had the reputation as being a woman who was reaching her breaking point. One of my friends saw her at the grocery store the day of the murder and told me that she looked angry and ready to pop. I just think she could not tolerate the cheating and lies anymore. Brandi also had a reputation of being a hothead. I had a dispute with her about her children hitting a baseball through my window and she just would not listen to me. I tried to talk to her calmly and explain to her that I only wanted her to pay for the window. Instead of talking, she screamed and yelled at me. She told me not to lecture her on how to raise her children. I think that is exactly what happened when she shot Chris. My guess is that she just would not listen to her husband's excuses and snapped.

I think it is common knowledge that Chris had issues with drugs, but nothing serious, just marijuana. I have seen some very disreputable people come by his house a few times when I was up late reading on my porch, especially in the last year or so. They would go in his house for only one or two minutes and then leave holding something in their hands. Everyone knew he liked to buy and sell small amounts of marijuana. I don't know if it means anything, but I found a very odd note in my car one day that stated, "Hey, if you need more to sell, let me know. C.A." I am positive the note fell out of Ricky's pocket because I just dropped him off at work, and it wasn't in my car when I picked him up. Also, although I don't know for sure, I think it was Chris Alexander's handwriting on the note.

On the night of Chris's murder, I was sound asleep in my bedroom when I heard what sounded like gunfire. It was so loud that I thought it was coming from my front yard. Concerned for my family's safety, I grabbed my .45 caliber gun and ran towards the window to see what was going on. I looked out the front window and didn't see anything in my yard or the Alexanders' yard across the street. I didn't hear anyone's house alarm going off. I certainly didn't see any car speeding away. The cops, including my brother Eric, came to my house to ask me questions about forty-five minutes after I heard the shots. I was completely truthful to them and told them everything I knew. I made sure to tell them about Chris and Brandi's reputations. In the end, I am positive that Brandi shot Chris. I just have this feeling about it that will not go away. I am normally never wrong about these things.

Signed: *Robert Hightower*

July 4, 20XX-2

Witnessed by: Detective Edwin Morris
Signed, *Edwin Morris*

July 8, 20XX-2

NL page 1 of 2

My name is Nikki Long. I hereby swear under penalty of perjury that the following is a true and accurate recounting of all relevant events that I can remember concerning my relationship with Chris Alexander and the time leading up to his death. I believe this statement to be a true and complete version of events as I remember them. I told my story to Detective Morris who then typed it up and let me review it.

My name is Nikki Long. I'm 25 years old. I own Nikki's Beauty Shop. I have been working there since I was 19. I actually met Chris, two years ago, while I was at the Salon. The day I met Chris is a day I will never forget. It was love at first sight. I was outside of the salon taking my 15 minute break, when all the sudden this fine, dark, tall, handsome man pulled up in the parking lot. He was on his way to Pro Style. Pro Style is a barber shop for men that's next door to Nikki's. When he walked by me he asked me for the time, and since I knew I had to make an impression I told him it was time for him to meet the girl of his dreams. Of course he laughed, and he actually missed that appointment he had for his hair cut. We sat outside and talked for about 2 hours. After that day Chris and I were in separable. Well almost, the only time we spent apart was when he had to go home to Brandi and the kids.

Brandi was jealous of me. Jealous that I'm younger, jealous that I'm prettier and thinner, jealous that her man loved and wanted me. It started to go downhill really bad with Chris and Brandi when she found out I was pregnant. When I found out I was going to have Chris's baby I couldn't keep it a secret. I told everyone at the salon that they were going to have to start planning my baby shower because I was about to be a mommy! I knew Brandi was going to find out about the baby because she was friends with people who came to Nikki's, and she got her hair done there a few times as well.

I ended up losing that baby and when that happened I didn't go to work for, like, 3 weeks. I was miserable, I was sad because Chris and I were finally going to have a child, we were going to be a family and I lost all that when I lost the baby. I didn't know if he would leave "her" once I lost the baby and worrying about that nearly broke my heart. When I finally decided to come back to work, Brandi was there getting her hair done. When she saw me, she said "sorry to hear about your loss, but good things never happen to bad people." I couldn't believe she said that to me. If I didn't love Chris so much, and have so much respect for his family, I would have slapped her right then and there. I did swear at her, calling her a bad word and promised her that she would "get" hers someday.

Chris's family is important in our town. His family is respected, and I would never want to do anything that would cause drama for them so I calmed down after I yelled at her. I just smirked at her and went to my station to get ready for the day. I felt like I shouldn't waste any more breath on Brandi, I had what she wanted. I had her man And I was keeping him too!

NL page 2 of 2

I told Chris about what Brandi said to me at my job, and he assured me not to worry about her. He said that Brandi did this to herself. He told me that Brandi did not have feelings for him anymore, and all she cared about was her own self-image. They weren't even sleeping in the same room. He would sleep on the couch, and the only reason he had not left her was because of the kids. And he promised me that it wouldn't be long until he left her for good and would marry me.

Chris and I were going to get married, and Brandi knew it. That's why she did what she did. On the night of Chris's murder, Chris went out with his brother. I was going to go out with them that evening, but I had 3 perms, and 2 press and curls that day and I was exhausted. I told Chris, to just call me on his way home so I knew he made it home safe. Chris always called to kiss me goodnight, so I waited by the phone. Chris called me while he was on his way home. He told me that he had stopped at Wendy's for a burger. Chris always got a burger and a drink before he went home. He seemed to have a lot of friends at the Wendy's. He told me that you should never go to sleep on an empty stomach, especially after drinking.

While we were on the phone, Chris told me that he wanted us to move in together. He said that he and Brandi got into an argument earlier that day, and he told her it was over. He said that he told her he would be leaving by the end of the week. I was so excited that Chris was finally leaving Brandi. I had been sharing Chris for two years, and finally he would be all mine. My conversation with Chris lasted around 35 minutes. I heard him use his keys to open the door, and I heard him reset the alarm to his house. I also heard him turn on the TV, and then he complained that his order was wrong. They put onions on his burger, and Chris hates onions. All of a sudden Chris then said "I'll call you back". I asked him is she in front of you, and he said yes. Whenever Chris would say I'll call you back, especially when he says it suddenly, then, that's my signal to just hang up, and I know he will call me back when Brandi leaves the room.

My Chris did not call me back that night. I never got my goodnight kiss from him. I learned that two minutes after we hung up he was killed. I guess she figured if she couldn't have him, then neither could I.

Signed: *Nikki Long*
        July 8, 20XX-2

Witnessed by: Detective Edwin Morris
Signed, *Edwin Morris*
July 8, 20XX-2

SB page 1 of 2

My name is Sharon Barry. I hereby swear under penalty of perjury that the following is a true and accurate recounting of all relevant events that I can remember concerning my interactions with Brandi and Chris Alexander.

I first met the defendant, <u>Brandi Alexander</u> about <u>six months</u> before Chris Alexander passed away. According to the insurance policy the date that we met was January 5, 20XX-2. At the time I worked for Friends Helping Friends (FHF) Insurance as an insurance agent. Currently, I am no longer employed with FHF Insurance. I work for another insurance company, as a supervising agent.

According to my notes, I was contacted by Chris Alexander in mid-December of 20XX-3 to meet with him and his wife. They were looking to purchase an insurance policy for Chris Alexander in the event that he passed away, so that he could make sure that his wife and children were taken care of financially. I specifically remember that it was Chris who called because I thought it was such a responsible thing for a husband and father to do.

The meeting on January 5, 20XX-2 took place at the Alexander' home. The meeting took place at 6 pm after both Brandi and Chris were home from work.   The meeting was routine. I received personal information from both Brandi and Chris regarding their ages, health, family history, and other insurance policies or health coverage. At that time, I was made aware that Chris had another insurance policy, which was issued by Chris's employer for roughly $80,000. We talked about all of their options, and I remember filling out a worksheet with them establishing that Chris was underinsured – not uncommon for folks his age by the way.

After completing all the relevant insurance forms, Brandi and Chris obtained coverage for Chris at $250,000. This insurance amount was based on the monthly cost of the policy. A higher insurance amount would have cost them more money each month, and they were unable to afford any higher coverage. The premium is based on all the personal information that was provided to me at the time. The premium amounts are pre-set based on the personal information. I followed the proper procedures outlined by FHF Insurance when providing the coverage amount and monthly cost.

At that time Brandi declined to insure herself. It was my understanding that Brandi and Chris made this decision after talking over the monthly cost of life insurance for either both of them, or just for one. I am unaware how or why this decision was reached. After providing them with an insurance quote, I allowed Brandi and Chris to talk about their decision in private. I went outside while they were talking in private, and they called me back into the house when they had made a decision. Chris signed the paperwork that day.

Chris listed Brandi, his wife, as his sole beneficiary.

SB page 2 of 2

I had no further contact with either Brandi or Chris until after Chris was killed. About 4 days after Chris died, Brandi called me. Brandi told me that Chris was murdered and that she needed to claim his life insurance. She qualified her desire for the life insurance collection in such a short period of time after his death, because she needed the money to help cover funeral expenses. This was not unusual, since funeral homes expect payment when services are rendered.

I immediately put the claim through to my superiors at FHF Insurance, and a check was ready within a few days. I called Brandi back that same day and told her that the claim was processing. We talked a long time. Brandi seemed so terribly distraught and in need of sympathy and attention. I asked Brandi if it was okay for me to come by and pay my respects. She told me where she was staying, since Chris died in her home, she said she was staying at her mother's house. Brandi told me she could not bear to go back into her house, the place where the love of her life was brutally murdered.

I took the next few days off of work and stayed by Brandi's side, along with her other friends and family. We became instantly close, and, as sad as this is, we bonded during her time of mourning. To this day we remain friends. We talk on the phone at least twice a week; we go to dinner and movies together.

I enjoy Brandi's company. She is such an honest, sweet, and caring person. It was devastating when she was charged with Chris's murder. There is no way she could have killed Chris. She only spoke fondly of him, regardless of his affairs. She knew that Chris loved her more than any other woman. She told me over and over again how she refused to leave her. Brandi is a wonderful mother too. Her children are well-behaved, polite and adorable. This is because Brandi has raised them properly, like a good-hearted woman would.

Signed: *Sharon Barry*

August 12, 20XX-2

Witnessed by: Detective Edwin Morris
Signed, *Edwin Morris*

August 12, 20XX-2

I remember the night Chris Alexander was killed. I don't remember the exact date, but I clearly remember what happened that night.. How could I forget? I've been Mr. and Mrs. Alexander' neighbor for about fifteen years. They were always such a nice couple. We would say hello in passing and Mr. Alexander sometimes mowed my lawn for me. Their children were always so polite. They where such a nice family... That's why it was such a shock to me when he was killed.

On the night Mr. Alexander was murdered I was on the phone with my aunt. My mom's 65th birthday was that coming weekend and my aunt and I were talking about the surprise party we were planning on throwing for her. Aunt Nancy is a bit old and hard of hearing so we were talking pretty loud. No matter though, I sure heard those gunshots. They were very loud. Scared me half to death they did. At first I didn't know what it was exactly. I thought it might have been a car backfiring, but they came so close together I knew it couldn't be that. It's just so unusual to hear gun shots in my neighborhood I didn't know what to do. That neighbor Mr. Hightower has fired his pistol in the neighborhood a time or two and it sounded a lot like that.

Next thing I know, I heard a car screeching out of the driveway next door. I was too afraid to go to the window and look, but I heard the car pull out of the driveway and head east away from my home. I would say the screeching happened only seconds later — it all happened so fast. I didn't go outside because I don't like to go out after dark. The cops never came by to talk with me about it and I thought they knew about the car. I called the DA's office to offer my help but they never came by either. As God is my witness this is my memory of the events that evening.

Signed: *Doris Presley*

-Notes-

Witness Name: Billy Bob Schifflett
Date Statement taken: August 14, 20xx-2
Investigator: Dana Stubbs

My name is Billy Bob Schifflett and I own the "From My Cold Dead Hands" Shootin' club in Pelican Bay. Well, actually we sit outside the city limits in Calusa County. We are really part of Gulfport, a small unincorporated place where folks can do what they like without the government interfering in our business. Gulfport has a long history of folks that like on the outskirts of society and we like it that way – for good reason.

I've owned the club for about 5 years now, I won in a poker game from a fellow that ain't around here no more. I pay my taxes, high though they are, and I don't cause nobody no trouble and I intends to keep it that way.

I don't remember who actually came into the Shooting club to use the range on the 25th of May, 20XX-2, but we do have specific procedures that the federal government requires us to follow and I've been following them since 911.

Whenever anyone comes in I make them take a short safety test, we give them a briefing and then check their ID to make certain that they are who they claim to be. They go downstairs to the shooting range to use it. We don't go downstairs with them, but we do control access to the shooting range area. All of our ranges, and we got 4 of them, are downstairs. Range 1 is a rifle range and the other three are for pistols. They are underground for safety reasons.

Once shooters get downstairs they have to sign in on our sign in sheet. I don't watch them do that, and they are on their own honor to do it. Gun owners are usually sticklers for following rules – it's a safety thing.

I know both Chris and Brandi Alexander. I went to school with them and Chris has bought quite a few guns from me over the years. He's bought pistols and rifles. I sold him a .45 caliber pistol about a year ago that was Army surplus. Brandi's come here with him once or twice, but I don't specifically remember seeing her anytime in the club in the last 6 months.

Chris has brought other people in her from time to time, but I did not go to school with any of them and did not recognize them. I don't think I could pick them out of a lineup, but one of them was definitely a young woman.

I have provided you guys with a copy of our sign in roster like you asked. I did close the range around 2 on the 25th of May 20XX-2. I waited till no one was using it. I don't remember how much brass we cleaned up that day and what type of guns were fired. You'd have to check the roster and talk to the folks on it. The brass was all destroyed. We have a company that comes by and picks it up for recycling.

Signed: *Billy Bob Schifflett*

NL page 1 of 1

My name is Nikki Long. I have thought a long time about what happened that awful night and I have more information that I need to tell you. I've been racking my brains trying to remember exactly what it was I heard and last night in a dream it came to me.

When Chris said "I'll call you back" I got angry at him. I'm ashamed to admit it but I had really been pissed at him for not leaving Brandi yet and I yelled at him. Yes, I know, I'm so ashamed to admit it but I yelled at my darling Chris in those last moments before he died. He started to say something and then I heard Brandi through the phone. She was yelling. I heard her say "Are you talking to that whore Nikki Long? I told you to stay away from that slut!"

Then I heard a door slam. Chris said to me "look baby I gotta...." And then all of a sudden I heard these loud banging sounds. Right after that I heard a gun go off several times and then I heard someone pick up the cell phone and the line went dead.

I hope she burns in Hell for taking Chris away from me that night.

Signed: *Nikki Long*

August 18, 20XX-2

Witnessed by: Detective Edwin Morris
Signed, *Edwin Morris*

July 8, 20XX-2

-Notes-

My name is Anece Baxter-White. I hereby swear under penalty of perjury that the following is a true and accurate recounting of all relevant events related to my involvement in this case. I have prepared this affidavit at the request of the prosecuting attorney in the case of *State v. Alexander*. I was the officer on the scene the night of Chris Alexander's murder. I have been a police officer for Calusa County for the past 15 years. During this time, I have investigated about 50 shootings, as well as numerous other violent crimes. I have been trained in the collection of evidence by the Calusa County Police Department.

On the night of June 3, 20XX-2, our department received a 911 call at 11:16 pm from the defendant's PDQ alarm service reporting a shooting. Myself and other officers were sent to the scene by our dispatch office. To my knowledge we did not receive a 911 call from the defendant herself. I arrived at the scene at some point after the call. I wrote in my report that I arrived at 11:01pm, but I know that this is incorrect, because we didn't receive the 911 call until 11:16pm. I was about 10 minutes away from the neighborhood when I received the call.

Outside of the home, I observed skid marks on the road in front of the defendant's driveway. The front of the home had nice landscaping, with several trees and rose bushes. It seemed like a nice upper-middle class neighborhood. A few neighbors were standing on their front lawns observing the situation. I directed another officer to interview some of the neighbors to search for leads. The defendant's front windows were closed, but the front drapes were open. When I approached the front door, I noticed several shell casings on the ground and heard the defendant crying. She appeared to be in distress; she was in the living room kneeling beside her husband's body, shaking him, and yelling at him to wake up. The paramedics had to pull her away from the body.

The body was located in the living room. The deceased was lying on his back, but it was unclear whether he had been standing or sitting when he was shot. Further inspection of the body revealed that the decedent had sustained multiple gun wounds, including two (2) shots to the groin area, which usually indicates a crime of passion. There were also two (2) bullets found in the concrete underneath the body, which could indicate that the gun was fired after the decedent had already fallen. The only blood present at the scene was that underneath the decedent, which lead me to believe he was not moved after death, and was shot and killed in the room he was found in. The bullets came from a .45 caliber gun. We turned the bullets over to ballistics for testing. Besides the bullets in the body, I also observed a bullet lodged in the doorway to the foyer. The positioning of the bullet indicated that the shooter was probably standing near the front door when they fired the gun. There were multiple bullet holes in the home. We retrieved several slugs, but the rounds fired were hollow points that broke apart on impact. I also discovered bullets in the interior walls of the living room and the foyer inside the home.

No viable samples for ballistics testing could be located and I cannot state with any degree of certainty the weapon that fired these rounds.

Upon further investigation of the house, I noticed the decedent's shirt and shoes in the living room. The television was turned on, and there was a bag of Wendy's food on the table. There was a small bag of marijuana and another of cocaine inside the takeout bag. It appeared that the decedent had been watching TV in the living room, was drawn to the foyer for some reason, then was shot. I also walked through out the house prior to speaking with Ms. Alexander. I looked at all of the windows and none appeared to have been broken or tampered with. I noted that the alarm system was activated and currently functioning. I then attempted to talk to Ms. Alexander but she was incredibly upset, weeping, screaming, almost howling.

When the defendant finally calmed down, I asked her what had happened. She told me she was asleep in her bed, and was awaken by a sound which she thought was her air conditioning. She smelt smoke and got up to investigate. She then observed the front door open, and saw her husband lying on the ground. She determined he was dead. She stated her PDQ alarm company called her, and they called 911 for her. I then asked her if she had a gun. She replied that she did not. However, when I searched the defendant's bedroom, I found an empty gun holster, belonging to a 9 mm gun, underneath the bed. I asked her again if she had a gun. This time she replied she did, and led me to a 9mm gun she kept high on a shelf in the laundry room. This gun used to shoot the decedent, a .45 caliber revolver, was not recovered.

The defendant's children were also home. They slept through the shooting, and did not wake up when myself and the detectives arrived. I found this to be unusual, because gun shots are loud, and the children's bedroom was in very close proximity to the living room. However, there was no evidence found at the scene to indicate that the children had been drugged. There did appear to be 8 empty Benadryl cellophane packets on the kitchen table but Ms. Alexander stated, and the parents of Chris Alexander verified, that the children had been sick with colds.

After about 3 hours of searching the home and interviewing the defendant, my team and I left. Once I got back to the station it was determined that a GSR test of the defendant's hands would be necessary. The test was conducted after the time we had left the home. We did not maintain constant supervision with the defendant between the time we left the scene and when the GSR test was conducted.

Anece Baxter-White

Anece Baxter-White
July 13, 20XX-1

IN THE CIRCUIT COURT OF THE FIRST JUDICIAL DISTRICT
CALUSA COUNTY
CRIMINAL DIVISION

State   )
)
)
)
)
v.   ) CASE NO.: 0318-20XX
)
)
)
Brandi Alexander   )
)

DEPOSITION OF: Roger Curlin

TAKEN BY: State

BEFORE: COURT REPORTER Vilma Rodriquez
                 PELICAN BAY COURT REPORTERS
                 2113 Veritas Way
                 PELICAN BAY, XX 33707

DATE: September 11, 20XX-2

LOCATION: Criminal Justice Center
                 6745 49th Avenue South
                 Pelican Bay, XX 33707

State Attorney Questioning Begins:

Q: Please state your name and Profession.

A: My name is Roger Curlin and I am a Forensic Scientist with
    the State Bureau of Investigation. I have held that
    position for the last fifteen years.

Q: What is your educational background?

A: I graduated from University of Phoenix with a Bachelor of Science in Biochemistry and received my Masters degree from the University of Phoenix.

Q: Do you have a doctorate?

A: No, I was working on my doctorate when I had some family issues, so I have not completed my dissertation in order to obtain my doctorate degree. I have done all the course work.

Q: What types of forensic science do you specialize in?

A: I do not specialize in any type of forensic science because I find that too restricting, instead I am broadly trained and skilled in a variety of forensic specialties.

Q: What investigative steps did you take involving the Alexander murder?

A: On June 3, 200x-2, I was summoned by the Pelican Bay Police Department to the home of Chris and Brandi Alexander. I conducted an initial examination of the crime scene and determined that the shooter in this case should have gunshot residue on their person and hands.

Q: What is a gunshot residue test?

A: A GSR test is the most common test performed to determine if a person was in the presence of gunshot residue within a limited time period after a weapon is discharged.

Q: How do you test for gunshot residue?

A: The test is pretty simple and the procedure is performed all over the United States and is admitted as evidence in many criminal cases. Like I said, the test is fairly simple. When someone fires a gun, the gun releases a pattern of particles that leave a residue. This residue is comprised of a combination of lead, barium, and antimony particles that are fused together. The same explosion that forces the bullet out of the gun also releases these particles into an invisible cloud that leaves traces of residue on the shooter's hand, surrounding area, and the victim's body. In order to determine if a person has fired a gun, the procedure is to swab the area of the suspect's hand to collect any residue present. Then, we analyze the swabs with a GSR machine that determines if the swab samples are positive for traces of GSR and, if so, to what extent.

Q: When do you test someone for GSR?

A: I test the individual or individuals the detective on the scene wishes to have tested. In this case, that would be the defendant, Brandi Alexander.

Q: Where was this test conducted?

A: At the Alexanders' residence. I tested Mrs. Alexander at her home. I swabbed both hands and placed the cotton swabs into two sterile bags; one for the left hand and one for the right hand. I noted that Mrs. Alexander's dominant hand was her right. I later performed the analysis, and I determined that there was at least one particle of GSR from the left hand swab taken from Mrs. Alexander.

Q: What do you need to ensure the most accurate results?

A: For the most accurate results, a GSR sample should be taken within five (5) hours of the initial gunshot. I performed the test on Mrs. Alexander within three (3) hours of the shooting, but if Mrs. Alexander washed her hands or had substantial contact with anything, the amount of GSR on her hands at the time of the swab would be reduced.

Q: Does the fact that you are not specifically trained in GSR testing affect the validity of your test results?

A: No. Although I do not have extensive expertise or education in the analysis or methodology of GSR, I did take the course that was offered by the manufacturer of the GSR machine we use to analyze the swabs. I do not think there is a need for any additional training, in fact, there is not really that much to know. Either there is GSR on the suspect or there is not, it is as simple as that. In my mind, if there is GSR present then the person must have fired a weapon recently. I am not aware of any studies that have dealt with other ways in which GSR might contaminate a scene, and I have not studied the predicted GSR patterns for types of weapons.

Q: You are qualified to conduct the test and record results?

A: Yes, that is a fair and accurate description of what I do.

Q: I have no further questions.

//Defense Counsel declined to question the witness during

the deposition//

-Notes-

IN THE CIRCUIT COURT OF THE FIRST JUDICIAL DISTRICT
CALUSA COUNTY
CRIMINAL DIVISION

State   )

v.   ) CASE NO.: 0318-20XX

Brandi Alexander   )

DEPOSITION OF: Dr. Jeremiah Jones

TAKEN BY: State

BEFORE: COURT REPORTER Vilma Rodriquez
                PELICAN BAY COURT REPORTERS
                2113 Veritas Way
                PELICAN BAY, XX 33707

DATE: September 12, 20XX-2

LOCATION: Criminal Justice Center
                6745 49th Avenue South
                Pelican Bay, XX 33707

State Attorney Questioning Begins:

Q: Please state your name and Profession.

A: My name is Dr. Jeremiah Jones, and I am both the County
Coroner and Medical Examiner for Calusa County. I have held
that position for the last twenty years.

Q: What is your educational background?

A: I graduated from State University with a Bachelor of
Science in chemistry and attended medical school in
Grenada. I completed my residency in 20XX-24. For the

first four years I worked in the emergency room of Calusa County Hospital and then became the county coroner in 20XX-20.

Q: Do you have any specializations?

A: Yes. I have conducted advanced studies in medical examiner training. I have also been on Court TV many times. They affectionately refer to me as Dr. Death on that show. I try to share my years of expertise with the audience.

Q: What types of forensic science do you specialize in?

A: I specialize in cause of death investigations. I am particularly adept at event reconstruction as determined by the placement, angle, velocity and burn mark patterns associated with gunshot wounds.

Q: What investigative steps did you take involving the Alexander murder?

A: I conducted the initial examination to determine the cause of death.

Q: How did you accomplish this?

A: I conducted an initial examination of Mr. Alexander's body when it was first brought into the county morgue. It was immediately obvious that he died from gunshot wounds to both the groin and chest. I determined that the manner of death was homicide and that the cause of death was by gunshot.

Q: What happened after you conducted this initial examination?

A: I put on my M.E. hat and got down to work. I performed an autopsy of Mr. Alexander in order to determine why he died.

Q: What did you determine?

A: I determined that Mr. Alexander was shot twice in the chest of 4 times in the groin. Based upon the pattern of blood splatter it was evident that the groin injuries occurred first.

Q: Is it really possible to determine that?

A: Absolutely. The flow of blood internally, when combined with the information provided by the investigating police officers made it clear. I don't even need to see any alleged blood splatter patterns to make this determination. The wounds in the body are the controlling factor when analyzing cause of death here.

Q: Which shots caused the death of Mr. Alexander?

A: Clearly the groin shots. It appears that he was shot in the groin, severing at least one femoral artery. He was then allowed to bleed for approximately 10 minutes, probably while being held at gunpoint. Once he had "bled out" a great deal the coup de grace was administered by shooting him twice in the chest.

Q: Doctor, to what degree of medical certainty can you state this opinion as to the cause of death?

A: I am completely certain of it. I would stake my reputation on it.

Q: I have no further Questions.

//Defense Counsel declined to question the witness during

the deposition//

DIRECT EXAMINATION

Defense Counsel Begins

Q: Mrs. Alexander, please introduce yourself to the jury.

A: My name is Brandi Alexander, and I am the defendant in this case.

Q: Tell us about yourself.

A: I am the youngest of three children. My parents always jokingly referred to me as their "little Einstein." I was really bookish and nerdy as a kid. Unlike most teens, I didn't really rebel, do drugs, or get into alcohol. I liked school and put my energies into doing well. My brother and sister always gave me a hard time about it. They used to joke that I was "old before my time."

Q: When did you first meet your husband?

A: I first met Chris in high school in 20XX-14. He was a year behind me in school.

Q: What do you remember about him then?

A: I remember he was popular, athletic, and liked girls and cars. Girls liked him, too, but the rumor was that he liked to love girls and then leave them. So, of course, I was a little worried when he started to date one of my girlfriends, Cynthia. They dated only for a short while during my senior year.

Q: What interaction did you have with him back then?

A: Chris and Cynthia had gone together to the senior prom. I remember that night pretty well, partially because my date had broken his leg that very same day and couldn't make it, and partly because Cynthia was angry with Chris because he wanted to stop by Wendy's before the dance. I laughed when she told me the story and she stormed off saying that I was naive and "didn't know anything" leaving Chris and me alone at the punch bowl.

Q: What happened then?

A: Chris seemed embarrassed and made some small talk. When he learned I didn't have a date for the evening, he didn't make me feel bad about not having a date and went out of his way to include me without hurting Cynthia's feelings. He was very nice to me. I remember thinking he was handsome, smart, and funny. He had a nice smile. Cynthia and I made up later that night. The three of us had a great time at the prom.

Q: When was the next time you got together with Chris?

A: Oh it was years later. Chris and I met again --oh, I think it was in May of 20XX-11. It was right before my college graduation. I had just had my hair done at the hair salon when I ran into him. He recognized me first. He told me he was going in to the barber shop next door to get a shave and a haircut. Other than a well-kept a goatee, Chris looked the same as he did in high school—he had that same easy smile.

Q: What did you two talk about?

A: We made some small talk and laughed about prom night. I told Chris that Cynthia had died last year from breast cancer. Chris said he knew her husband well and that he had visited Cynthia at home a few times before she had passed. We discussed how Cynthia had turned to medical use of marijuana to ease her pain, even though it had not been prescribed for her. Chris said he heard that too, and agreed that Cynthia's last weeks had been sad and tragic.

Q: Did you see him again?

A: Yes. When Chris suggested we have lunch together sometime, I mentioned there wasn't a Wendy's for several miles and said I didn't like their Frosties. Chris laughed. He said he loved Wendy's and would forgive me that. He also joked that he understood now that Wendy's was off-limits for a "first date"—he learned that much from prom night. Then he asked for my number and promised to call me, which he did later that night. We made a date for the following weekend and dated for several months afterward.

Q: Were you working then?

A: No, but shortly thereafter I got a job as an elementary school teacher after graduation. I taught third grade at Pelican Bay Elementary School, only four blocks from my parents' home.

Q: Did Chris work?

A: Unlike me, Chris never went to college after high school. He always told me that college wasn't his "thing." Although most of his family was in law enforcement or civil service, Chris always told me that he preferred to work with his hands and he couldn't stand the idea of being in a job where people told him what to do just because they outranked him. He said he "gave up the chance to join the Army" for that very reason and went to trade school instead. After graduating from trade school, Chris had landed a good job as a tool and die maker for Industrial Metal Fabrication (IMF) Company, less than a mile from my parents' home. He said the flexible swing-shift hours, high hourly pay, union protection, and benefits suited him well.

Q: Did your husband have a lot of contacts in the community?

A: While we were dating, Chris always ran into people he knew. Although they were friendly with Chris, none of them really seemed to know him that well. The women we ran into made me nervous—they were very forward with Chris and touched him a lot, which was not my style. Chris would tell me not to mind the other girls—that I was the one for him. He said he liked that I was "old fashioned" and looked out for him, and he never let anyone, man or woman, get too close. He said that friends were less important to him than family, and I was family. I liked that he worried about what I thought. His popularity made me feel important and proud of him.

Q: What did your family think of him?

A: My family liked Chris well enough. My mom never seemed to warm up to him, though. I just figured it was my mom being a mom—she was always protective of me and my siblings. My brother and sister lived in town, but met Chris only two times before Chris and I were married. They all got along fine. Chris and I were married on December 20, 200x-10. Chris and I never had sex before marriage—mostly because we agreed it should be that way. Chris respected who I was and I never felt otherwise.

Q: How did you get along with his family?

A: Good most of the time. Chris had a large extended family—blood relatives, distant cousins, and friends of the family made up the majority of his social network. They were very different from my own family in that they distrusted outsiders and seemed "larger than life."

Q: How did you adjust to his family?

A: Well, you know ,Chris was different around them. He talked loudly and irreverently. Chris was always the center of attention and seemed to lose himself in the attention they lavished on him. They called Chris often—at home, on his cell. There seemed to be no boundaries among them, except one: Chris always insisted that people call him before they dropped by the house. This was Chris's golden rule, and no one ever violated it. They usually called Chris on his cell, but it was not unusual for people to call the house as well.

Q: Was there anything else about Chris's behavior that seemed strange to you?

A: It was not unusual for Chris to head out in the middle of the night to have drinks, play cards, or hang out with "his family." Chris said it was just how his family was. He said if I just accepted that, his family would eventually warm up to me. They never really did though.

Q: How did you feel around his family?

A: Actually, I never really felt comfortable around Chris's family—especially around Chris's brother Willie. Willie drank too much and made me feel uncomfortable around him. One time, at a family picnic, both Willie and Chris had been drinking. They'd gone off together for a while, leaving me to help Chris's mom and cousins to clean up. When Chris and Willie returned, I smelled the faint odor of marijuana on them both. No one else seemed to notice. No one said a word. On the way home, when I asked Chris about it, he became angry with me. He left the house and did not come home for three days. When Chris returned, we never spoke about it again. In order to maintain peace in our home I accepted that I would never question Chris's behaviors around his family again, so long as Chris continued to treat me with respect.

Q: Did there come a time when Chris' work situation changed? Tell us about that.

A: About two years after we married, Chris's shifts became erratic at work. He was working long hours, two shifts a day. Although I missed spending time with him, he said the money was too good to pass up. He said it would help us save money and buy a large home.

Q: How did all these extra hours affect your family life?

A: The hours began to take their toll on Chris, I guess on me, too. He became resentful, and angry, he told me he had changed his mind about having children. He said he didn't want to feel "tied down"—I was devastated. Although we had been using protection and had agreed to wait until I was tenured to start a family, we had always planned to have children. Around this time I accidentally got pregnant. Chris became distant and angry at first, but one day, just seemed to "snap out of it."

Q: What happened next?

A: We bought a spacious three-bedroom home in an upper-class neighborhood in Pelican Bay, West Calusa Hills on Lullaby Lane, just before our first daughter, Ariel, was born. About two years later, I gave birth to our second daughter, Jasmine. Chris adored them. Even though Chris still worked long hours and came home late at night at least three or four times a week, he seemed a changed man. Chris was a devoted husband and father.

Q: Why did you have an alarm system at your house?

A: Shortly after we moved into our new home, we contracted with PDQ to install a monitored alarm system. Having the system made me feel much more secure, given that Chris's work hours sometimes involved his coming home late.

Q: Were there any weapons in the home?

A: Chris had a gun. Because Chris won't buy a gun safe, I make him keep it in the laundry room—on a high shelf out of the girl's sight and reach. It's the only way I can forget it's there and not worry about it being in the home.

Q: Why did you get life insurance on your husband recently?

A: One of Chris' friends put us in contact with Sharon Barry, a Friends Helping Friends (FHF) Insurance agent. Sharon set up a meeting with us, and agreed to come to our home to accommodate Chris's schedule. Sharon recommended we purchase a $250,000 policy, based on what we could afford at the time. A part of the insurance policy was assigned to pay funeral costs in the event of one of our deaths. We felt that this policy, plus the group policy Chris had through IMF would be more than ample to cover our family's needs.

Q: I would like to draw your attention now the night your husband was murdered. Do you remember that night?

A: I remember the night Chris was killed. I remember pieces—
some of it is vivid and clear in my mind. Other parts of it
are fragmented.

Q: Please explain.

A: June 3, 200x-2 was a Thursday evening. School had let out
for the summer a few weeks earlier. Around 10:00 PM, I
received a call from my niece, Lilli Duke. We discussed our
plans to meet for lunch the next day and only talked about
one minute. After hanging up the phone, I went to check on
the girls. They were sound asleep. The girls are like
their father—they can sleep through a live marching band
playing in their bedroom. Although I don't specifically
remember checking the alarm before going to bed, it was
usually my habit to do so. I hate being alone in the house
with the girls when Chris isn't home.

Q: What did you do next?

A: I took a bath and got ready for bed. I think I was asleep
by 10:30—bathing relaxes me. I have always been an early
bird, but something of a light sleeper. Chris usually slept
in the den when he got home late so he wouldn't wake me.
Chris wasn't home by the time I fell asleep.

Q: Did you stay asleep?

A: No, something startled me awake. I am still not certain if I
know exactly what it was. At first, I thought the noise
might be the air conditioner outside our bedroom window. The

fan and motor always makes noise when it kicks on, sort of

like a clack, loud hum, and then a pop, pop, pop. It drives

Chris crazy. I've learned to sleep through it or ignore it.

Q: What was the noise?

A: I don't know, but I don't think it was the air conditioner.

At least I don't think so. Before I realized what was

happening, I was in the living room. I saw Chris's body on

the floor. The alarm was sounding. The front door was open.

Chris was half dressed. He was not moving. I think I

screamed. I remember yelling at him—pounding on him to wake

up. I did not move from Chris's side. I think I was there

when the police arrived. It felt like an eternity. Later, I

learned it only took them a few minutes to arrive.

Q: What happened after the police arrived?

A: I don't really remember, I just remember questions being

asked of me. After I knew the girls were safe, I just zoned

out. There were police and technicians all over our home.

It was noisy. I don't even know what I was thinking, other

than I wanted to go somewhere safe with my girls. I remember

vaguely that the police asked me about guns in the house. I

think I told them there were no guns because I had forgotten

about the one in the laundry room. When the police showed me

a holster they found under the bed, I remembered the gun in

the laundry room and took them to it.

Q: How long did this questioning by the police last?

A: I'm not real sure, but after several hours, the police allowed me, Ariel, and Jasmine to leave the house with my brother. The police didn't search me before leaving, but, later, they called me back to the house and tested my hands and arms for gunpowder. The test turned out a single speck of gunpowder on the back of my left hand. Even though I told the police I did not kill my husband and that I was right-handed, they did not seem to believe me. I was arrested for the murder of my husband, Chris Alexander. My life, as I had once known it to be, ended forever.

Q: Ms. Alexander did you kill you husband?

A: No.

Q: Well if you didn't whom do you suspect?

A: I think it might have been that "lady" Nikki Long, she was mad because Chris had broken things off with her and come back home to me and the girls. He always came back to us. She had been talking crap around town about how she was going to take my man and I know that sort of stuff embarrasses his family - you just don't want to make them mad.

Q: Nothing further, Your Honor.

Certificate of Death

Name	Sex	Hour of Death	Date of Death
Chris Alexander	M	2300 hours	**6/6/20XX-2**

Race	Age	DOB	County of Death
Other	36	10/22/20XX-36	Calusa

SSN	Marital Status	Surviving Spouse	State of Death
555-45-3244	Married	Brandi Alexander	XX

Residence-State	Residence-County	Residence-City	Street Address
XXXXXXX	Calusa	Pelican Bay	6731 Lullaby Lane

Father	Mother	Address(es):
Willie Alexander	Frances Alexander	9123 South St., Pelican Bay, XX 33465

Informant's Name	Mailing Address:
Brandi Alexander	6731 Lullaby Lane, Pelican Bay, XX 33707

Disposition:	Cemetery/Crematorium	Location:	Medical Examiner:
Buried	Happy Acres	Pelican Bay	*Dr. Jeremiah Jones, M.E*

Funeral Home:	Mailing Address:
Happy Acres	P.O. Box 345, Pelican Bay, XX 33902

Person who pronounced death:	Pronounced Dead on:	Location:
Dr. Jeremiah Jones County Coroner/Medical Examiner	6/6/20XX-2	Calusa County Hospital 1921 Sherman Way Pelican Bay, XX 33450

Coroner:	Mailing Address:
Dr. Jeremiah Jones	Calusa County Hospital 1921 Sherman Way, Pelican Bay, XX 33450

Cause of Death:	Signature of Coroner:
Internal injuries from gunshot wounds to the chest and groin. Victim bled to death	*Dr. Jeremiah Jones, M.E.*

Other Significant Conditions:	Autopsy:	Was Case Referred to Medical Examiner:
4 non-lethal gunshot wounds	Yes	Yes

Accident/Suicide/Homicide/Other:	Means of Death:
Homicide	Gunshot wounds, Loss of Blood

Place of Death:	Address:
Home	6731 Lullaby Lane Pelican Bay, XX 33707

OFFICE OF THE MEDICAL EXAMINER
CALUSA COUNTY
Jeremiah Jones, M.D.
Eric Kilhim, M.D.
Carol Morbid, M.D.
505 South Morte Circle
Pelican Bay, XX 33333
(505) 555-0001

NAME: Chris Alexander   **AUTOPSY NO**: 00XX-2-767
SEX: Male   **DATE OF AUTOPSY**: Jun 8, 00XX-2
RACE: White   **TIME OF AUTOPSY**: 10:15 a.m.
AGE: 36   **PATHOLOGIST**: Jeremiah Jones, M.D.
DOB: 10/22/1771   Chief Medical Examiner

FINAL PATHOLOGICAL DIAGNOSES:

I.   MASSIVE HEMORRHAGING FROM SEVERED RIGHT FEMORAL ARTERY

II.   MASSIVE HEMORRHAGE FROM SEVERED LEFT FEMORAL ARTERY

III.   HEMORRHAGE IN RIGHT ANTERIOR GROIN AREA

IV.   HEMORRHAGE IN LEFT ANTERIOR GROIN AREA

V.   HEMORRHAGE IN LEFT CENTRAL CHEST AREA

CAUSE OF DEATH: MULTIPLE GUNSHOT WOUNDS TO THE GROIN AREA

MANNER OF DEATH: HOMICIDE

Dr. Jeremiah Jones, M.D.
Jeremiah Jones, M.D.
Chief Medical Examiner

CLOTHING:

The body has a pair of boxer underwear on, soaked with blood in the groin area. No other clothing items. No jewelry.

EXTERNAL EXAMINATION:

The body is that of a well-developed, well-nourished white male appearing the offered age of 38 years old. The body measures 74 feet and weighs 195 pounds.

The unembalmed body is well preserved and cool to touch due to refrigeration. Rigor mortis is developing in the major muscle groups. Liver mortis is fixed and purple posteriorly except over pressure points. During initial examination, there was no rigor and lividity was at a minimum and unfixed.

There are six gun shot wounds. All six wounds enter the body in the anterior and exit the body in the posterior. Two wounds are in the right chest area and four in the groin area. The wounds are described in detail below.

The scalp hair is black and measures up to 4 inches in length in the fontal area and up to 3 inches in the back and on top of the head. The irises are black and the pupils are dilated with redness. The teeth are natural and in good condition. The fenula are intact. The oral mucosa and tongue are free of injuries. The external ears have no injuries.

The neck is symmetrical and shows no masses or injuries. The trachea is in the midline. The shoulders are symmetrical and are free of scars.

The flat abdomen has no injuries. The back is symmetrical. The buttocks are unremarkable.

The fingernails are short and clean.

OTHER IDENTIFYING FEATURES:

There is one scar and one tattoo on the body.

SCAR:
There is ¼ inch scar on the top right arm anterior of the elbow.

TATTOOS:
There is one tattoo of the word "Frosty" on the right arm posterior of the shoulder. There is another tattoo of a marijuana leaf on the left arm posterior of the shoulder.

INTERNAL EXAMINATION:

The body was opened with the usual Y incision. The left chest and groin areas displayed significant trauma from gun shots. Otherwise, unremarkable.

BODY CAVITIES:

The muscles of the right chest were normal and the muscles of the left chest were torn and traumatized form the gun shots. The lungs were atelectatic when the pleural cavities were opened. The ribs, sternum and spine exhibit no fractures. The right pleural cavity was free of fluid. The left pleural cavity contained a moderate amount of blood. The pericardial sac has a normal amount of clear yellow fluid. The diaphragm has no abnormality. The subcutaneous abdominal fat measures 5 centimeters in thickness at the umbilicus. The abdominal cavity is lined with glistening serosa and has no collections of free fluid. The organs are normally situated. The mesentery and omentum are unremarkable.

NECK:

The soft tissues and the strap muscles of the neck exhibit no abnormalities. The hyoid bone and the cartilages and the larynx and thyroid are intact and show no evidence of injury. The larynx and trachea are lined by smooth pink-tan mucosa, are patent and contain no foreign matter. The epiglottis and vocal cords are unremarkable. The cervical verbal column is intact. The carotid arteries and jugular veins are unremarkable.

CARDIOVASCULAR SYSTEM:

The heart and great vessels contain dark red liquid blood and little postmortem clots. The heart weighs 308 grams. The epicedial surface has normal amount of glistening, yellow adipose tissue. The coronary arteries are free of atherosclerosis.

The pulmonary trunk and arteries are opened in situ and there is no evidence of thromboemboli. The intimal surface of the aorta is smooth with a few scattered yellow atheromata. The ostia of the major branches are normal distribution and dimension. The inferior vena cava and tributaries have no antemortem clots.

RESIRATORY SYSTEM:

The lungs weigh 555 grams and 552 grams, right and left respectively. There is a small amount of subpleural anthracotic pigment within the lobes. The pleural surfaces are free of exudates: right-sided pleural adhesions have been described above. The trachea and bonchi have smooth tan epithelium. The cut surfaces of the lungs are red-pin and have mild edema. The lung parenchyma is of the usual consistency and shows no evidence of neoplasm, consolidation, thromboemboli, fibrosis o calcification.

HEPATOBILIAY SYSTEM:

The liver weighs 2545 grams. The liver edge is somewhat blunted. The capsule is intact. The cut surfaces are red-brown and normal consistency. There are no focal lesions. The gallbladder contains 15 milliliters of dark green bile. There are no stones. The mucosa is unremarkable. The large bile ducts are patent and non-dilated.

HEMOLYMPHATIC SYSTEM:

The thymus is not identified. The spleen weighs 305 grams. The capsule is shiny, smooth and intact. The cut surfaces are firm and moderately congested. The lymphoid tissue in the spleen is within a normal range. The lymph nodes throughout the body are no enlarged.

GASTROINTESTINAL SYSTEM:

The tongue shows a small focus of sub mucosal hemorrhage near the tip. The esophagus is empty and the mucosa is unremarkable. The stomach contains an estimated 29 milliliters of thick sanguinous fluid. The gastric mucosa shows no evidence of ulceration. There is a mild flattening of the rugal pattern within the antrum with intense hyperemia. The duodenum contains bile-stained hick tan fluid. The jejunum, ileum, and the colon contain yellowish fluid with a thick, cloudy, particulate matter. There is no major alteration to internal and external inspection and palpitation except for a yellowish/white shiny discoloration of the mucosa. The vermiform appendix is identified. The pancreas is tan, lobulated and shows no neoplasia calcification or hemorrhage. There are no intraluminal masses or pseudomenbrane.

UROGENITAL SYSTEM:

The kindeys are similar size and shape and weigh 159 grams and 176 grams, right and left, respectively. The capsules are intact and strip with ease. The cortical surfaces are purplish, congested and mildly granular. The cut surfaces reveal a well-defined corticomedullary unction. There are no structural abnormalities of the medullae, calyces or pelvis. The ureters are slender and patent. The urinary bladder has approximately 0.5 milliliters of cloudy yellow urine. The mucosa is unremarkable.

The penis and testes appear normal.

ENDOKRINE SYSTEM:

The adrenal glands have a normal configuration with the golden yellow cotices well demarcated from the underlying medullae and there is no evidence of hemorrhage. The thyroid gland is mildly fibrotic and has vocally pale gray parenchyma on sectioning. The pituitary gland is within normal limits.

MUSCULOSKELETAL SYTEM:

Postmortem radiographs of the body show no acute, healed or healing fractures of the head, neck appendicular skeleton or the axial skeleton. The muscles are normally formed.

CENTRAL NERVOUS SYSTEM:

The scalp has no hemorrhage or contusions. The calvarium is intact. There is no epidural, subdural or subarachnoid hemorrhage. The brain has a normal convolutional pattern and weighs 1270 grams. The meninges are clear. The cortical surfaces of the brain have mild to moderate flattening of the gyri with narrowing of the sulci.

EVIDENCE OF INJURIES:

There are six gunshot wounds. These are given Roman Numeral designations; however these designations are random and do not correspond to the degree of severity of injuries, nor to the sequence in which they have been inflicted.

I.   Perforating gunshot wound of right upper chest:

An entrance gunshot wound is located on the decedent's right upper chest, 2 inches to the right of the right nipple. It is a 1/4 inch circular perforation with a symmetrical 1/8 inch dark margin of abrasion. No soot or stippling is seen in association with this wound.

After perforating the skin and soft tissues of the right chest, the bullet enters the right chest wall at the 5th intercostals space and subsequently fractures ribs #6-9, posterior-laterally and exits behind the right posterior chest wall through the 8th intercostal space. Powder residue is not visible in the wound track. There is moderate tissue disruption along the bullet track. There is no major or minor injury to any organ from this wound. No bullet is recovered.

This was an indeterminate/distant range perforating gunshot wound of the right chest which passes front to back, slightly left, and slightly downward.

II.   Perforating gunshot wound of right lower chest:

An entrance gunshot wound is located in the decedent's right lower chest, 2 inches below and 1 inch to the right of the right nipple. It is a 1/4 inch round perforation with an asymmetric margin of abrasion which measures 1/4 inch at the superior aspect of the wound and 1/8 inch at the inferior aspect of the wound. No soot or stippling is seen in association with this wound.

After perforating the skin and soft tissues of the left lateral chest, the bullet enters the abdominal cavity via the 8th intercostals space, injures multiple loops of small bowel and penetrates the retroperitoneal soft tissues of the upper left pelvis. The bullet exits the left lower back. Powder residue is not visible in the wound track. There is slight tissue disruption along the bullet track. No bullet is recovered.

This was an indeterminate/distant range gunshot wound of the right chest which passes front to back and downward.

III.   Perforating gunshot wounds of left groin:

There are two entrance gunshot wounds in the decedent's left pelvis area.

a. The first wound in the left groin area is located 1 inch to the left of the pubis. It is a 1/4 inch circular perforation with a symmetrical 1/8 inch dark margin of abrasion. No soot or stippling is seen in association with this wound. After perforating the skin, the wound extends through the muscles and soft tissues of the abdomen and punctures the prostate gland. The bullet perforates the psoas muscle and exits the body to the left of the sacrum.

b. The second wound in the left groin area is located 2 inches to the left of the pubis. It is a 1/4 inch circular perforation with a symmetrical 1/8 inch dark margin of abrasion. No soot or stippling is seen in association with this wound. After perforating the skin, the wound extends through the muscles and soft tissue of the abdomen and perforates the femoral artery. The bullet exits the body through the gluteus maximus to the left of the sacrum.

These are indeterminate/distant range gunshot wounds of the left groin which pass from front to back.

IV.   Perforating gunshot wounds of right groin:

There are two gunshot wounds in the decedent's right pelvis area.

a.   The first wound is in the right groin area located 1 and ¼ inches to the right of the pubis. It is a 1/4 inch circular perforation with a symmetrical 1/8 inch dark margin of abrasion. No soot or stippling is seen in association with this wound. After perforating the skin, the wound extends through the muscles and soft tissues of the abdomen and punctures the bladder. The bullet exits the body through the gluteus maximus to the right of the sacrum.

b. The second wound is in the right groin area located 3 inches to the right of the pubis. It is a 1/4 inch circular perforation with a symmetrical 1/8 inch dark margin of abrasion. No soot or stippling is seen in association with this wound. After perforating the skin, the wound extends through the muscles and soft tissues of the abdomen and punctures the right femoral artery. The bullet exits through the gluteus maximus to the left of the sacrum.

These are indeterminate/distant range gunshot wounds of the left groin which pass from front to back.

Enclosure 1 – Autopsy Diagram
Enclosure 2 – Blank Body Diagram

ST/GPS/lsr
Dictated: 06/08/00XX-2
Transcribed: 06/09/00XX-2
Finalized: 06/15/00XX-2

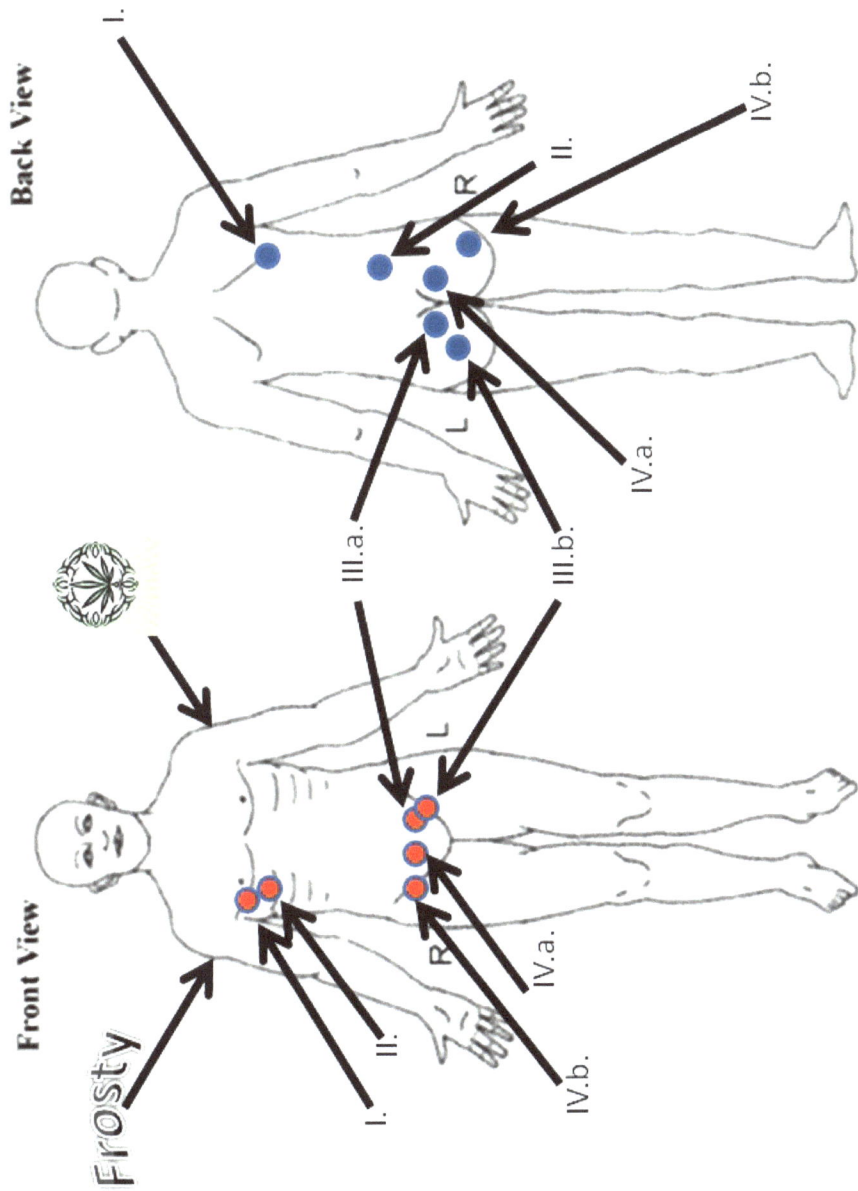

Back View

Front View

Frosty

I.

II.

R

IV.b.

L

IV.a.

III.a.

III.b.

II.

I.

R

IV.a.

IV.b.

L

Autopsy Notes: Chris Alexander, conducted 06/09/20XX-2

J.J. ME

Enclosure 2

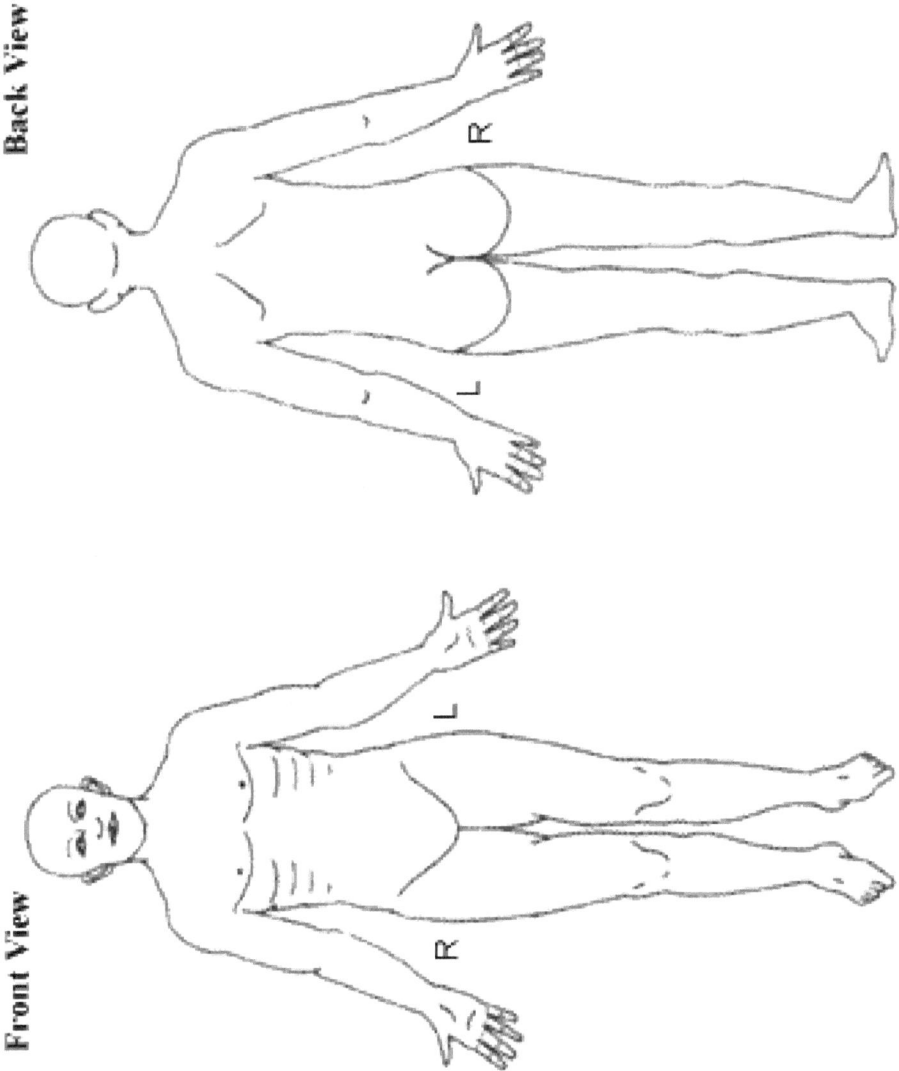

EVIDENCE

Agency:	Pelican Bay Police Department	Calusa County
Collected By:	Officer Anece Baxter-White	
Item Number:		Case Number: 20XX(-2)1959
Date:	6-6-20XX-2	Time: 2345 hours
Description:	Small Bag of white powder, field test positive for presence of cocaine, identified as exhibit 9 in the case file.	
Remarks:	Secured properly, carried to station and turned over to the evidence custodian.	

CHAIN OF CUSTODY

Received From:	Officer Anece Baxter-White *Anece Baxter-White*
Received By:	Detective William Murphy *Bill Murphy*
Date:	6-7-20XX(-2)	Time:	0239 HOURS

Received From:	Detective William Murphy – by Certified Mail
Received By:	Doctor Steven Schwarz, Calusa County Forensic Laboratory Felix Schwarz
Date:	7-23-20XX(-2)	Time:	0932 Hours

Received From:	Calusa County, Forensic Laboratory –by Certified Mail
Received By:	Detective William Murphy *Bill Murphy*
Date:	10-10-20XX(-2)	Time:	1232 Hours

EVIDENCE

Agency:	Pelican Bay Police Department	Calusa County
Collected By:	Officer Scott Frost	
Item Number:		Case Number: 20XX(-2)1959
Date:	6-6-20XX-2	Time: 0232 hours

Description: Small Bag of green leafy substance, field test positive for presence of marijuana, identified as exhibit 10 in the case file.

Remarks: Secured properly, carried to station and turned over to the evidence custodian.

CHAIN OF CUSTODY

Received From:	Officer Scott Frost *Scott Frost*
Received By:	Detective William Murphy *Bill Murphy*
Date:	6-7-20XX(-2) Time: 0339 HOURS
Received From:	Detective William Murphy – by Certified Mail
Received By:	Doctor Steven Schwarz, Calusa County Forensic Laboratory *Felix Schwarz*
Date:	7-23-20XX(-2) Time: 0932 Hours
Received From:	Calusa County, Forensic Laboratory –by Certified Mail
Received By:	Detective William Murphy *Bill Murphy*
Date:	10-10-20XX(-2) Time: 1232 Hours

CALUSA COUNTY FORENSIC LABORATORY

415 COUNTY ROAD 369

CALUSA COUNTY, FLORIDA 33459

August 4, 20XX-2

DRUG CHEMISTRY DIVISION REPORT

SUBJECT: Submitter Case Number: **20XX(-2)-9x-PBPD454**

 Laboratory Referral Number: 20XX(-2)-948

Subject: Chris Alexander

Exhibits:

1. 1 plastic bag containing white powder (Item 1)
2. 1 plastic bag containing green leafy substance (Item 2)

Findings:

Examination of white powder material in Exhibit 1 revealed the presence of cocaine. Amounts (grams):

Exhibit	Received	Used	Returned
1	45.0	0.5	44.5

Examination of green leafy substance material in Exhibit 2 revealed the presence of marijuana. Amounts (grams):

Exhibit	Received	Used	Returned
2	154.0	1.0	153.0

Stephen F. Schwarz, M.D.

Stephen F. Schwarz, Ph.D.
Forensic Chemist

CERTIFICATE

I certify that I am the custodian of records of the Calusa County Forensic Laboratory, and that the foregoing is a true copy of the record of this Laboratory.

James Holder, M.D.

JAMES HOLDER, M.D.
Director, Calusa County Forensic Laboratory

-Notes-

2914 49th Avenue South
Pelican Bay, XX 33606
727-555-9012

Mr. Christopher Alexander
6731 Lullaby Lane
Pelican Bay, XX 33707

Dear Sir/Ma'am:

In accordance with your *PDQ* Alarm system plan we are writing to inform you of the reported activity for your system during the time period May 15, 20XX-2 through June 15, 20XX-2. A review of the computer logs maintained on our system provides the following information:

Date:	Incident:	Action Taken:
20XX-2.05.16.2139	Alarm tripped – garage door	Called home IAW plan requirements. Homeowner Alexander answered phone call and indicated he had just come in through the garage and forgot to reset the system.
20XX-2.05.23.1649	Alarm tripped – front door	Called home IAW plan requirements. Homeowner's wife said children went out the door before the system was disarmed. Explained the fact that there is no lag time between opening of door and tripping of alarm.
20XX-2.06.06.2253	Alarm tripped – front door	Called home IAW plan requirements. Wife on the phone saying someone shot husband, send help. Very upset, almost incomprehensible. Called Police through 911 system and reported incident.

As always we appreciate your business and look forward to providing for all of your security related needs in the future.

Sincerely,

Russell Martin

Russell Martin
CEO, PDQ Alarm Systems

Individual Charges

Customer	Account Number	Invoice Period	Page
Chris Alexander	0166000555-3	May 31 – Jun 30	5 of 16

Individual Charges for   Chris Alexander (continued)

727-555-2260

cafrostie@sprintpcs.com

Voice Call Detail

Date	Time	Phone Number	Call Destination	Rate/ Type	Minutes Used	Airtime Charges	LD/Additional Charges	Total Charges
5.31	1739	555-3624	Pelican Bay	📟	7	included	0.00	0.00
5.31	1943	555-3461	Incoming		2	included	0.00	0.00
6.1	1345	555-3327	Pelican Bay		12	included	0.00	0.00
6.1	1603	555-3463	Jacksonville		3	included	0.00	0.00
6.1	1954	555-3461	Incoming		2	included	0.00	0.00
6.2	1433	555-6633	Pelican Bay		15	included	0.00	0.00
6.2	1729	555-3624	Pelican Bay	📟	29	included	0.00	0.00
6.3	2012	555-3327	Pelican Bay		5	included	0.00	0.00
6.3	2213	555-1623	Incoming		2	included	0.00	0.00
6.5	2312	555-3463	Jacksonville		4	included	0.00	0.00
6.6	1501	01934-679	Juarez, Mx		2	included	0.00	0.00
6.6	1515	555-1623	Incoming		2	included	0.00	0.00
6.6	1621	555-3461	Incoming		2	included	0.00	0.00
6.6	1752	01934-679	Mexico City, Mx		2	included	0.00	0.00
6.6	2201	555-5172	Pelican Bay		4	included	0.00	0.00
6.6	2210	555-3624	Pelican Bay	📟	23	included	0.00	0.00

📟 - LTE Call

EM Notes:

555-5172 – Alexander Home Number

555-3327 – Brandi Alexander Cell Phone

555-3624 – Nikki Long Cell Phone

555-6633 – Nikki's Hair Salon

Doctor Horrible

The Pelican Bay Star

November 3, 20XX-2
By Phillip Payne, State Court Correspondent

In January, the State Supreme Court took an unusual step. In the murder trial of 14-year-old Danny Wayne Morris, the court tossed out the testimony of the medical examiner who had conducted the autopsy of the body.

Why you may ask? The medical examiner in the case, Dr. Jeremiah Jones, had testified under oath that he could tell from the bullet wounds in the body that Morris and his brother simultaneously held the gun to fire the fatal shot. Unfortunately it is impossible to make such a determination from examining bullet wounds, a point the Supreme Court explained at length in their opinion.

Former Pelican Bay Police Chief B.J. Mills has been trying for years to draw attention to Dr. Jones. "There's no question in my mind that there are innocent people doing time due to the testimony of Dr. Jones," he says. "I reckon some may even be on death row."

Over the twenty years that Dr. Jones has been a medical examiner state Supreme Court justices, police officers, defense lawyers, crime lab experts and other state medical examiners have made public their concerns with his practice at one time or another.

Although Dr. Jones refused to speak talk with the paper, he did make the following observation on the witness stand during the Morris trial. He claimed under oath to perform anywhere from 1,500 to 1,800 autopsies a year. The National Association of Medical Examiners (NAME) says a medical examiner should perform no more than 250 autopsies per year. After 325, the organization refuses to certify an examiner's practice.

"That number cannot be done," says Antonio DeMarossa, author of The Complete Guide to Forensic Pathology, widely considered the guiding textbook. "After 250 autopsies, you start making small mistakes. At 300, you're going to get mental and physical strains on your body. Over 350, and you're talking about major fatigue and major mistakes."

For much of his career Dr. Jones, 71, has conducted autopsies as well as held two research and hospital positions and testified in court two to four times per week. After reviewing one Jones autopsy in a 2003 homicide case, Dr. James McDonald, who sits on NAME's ethics committee, sent a strongly-worded letter to the defendant's attorney describing Dr. Jones's conclusions as "near-total speculation," the quality of his report "pathetic." As a result of Dr. McDonald's letter, the prosecutor dropped the murder charge and the defendant pleaded guilty to the lesser charge of manslaughter.

Another medical examiner reviewed Dr. Jones's autopsy in a 1998 homicide and characterized his work as "near complete malpractice." In that case, Dr. Jones had determined that a woman had died of "natural causes." The diagnosis was later changed to homicide by blunt force to the head. According to the medical examiner that performed the second autopsy, Dr. Jones hadn't even emptied the woman's pockets, a standard autopsy procedure. No one has been prosecuted in the case. Dr. Jones declined repeated requests from me to comment.

Dr. Jones isn't a board-certified forensic pathologist, at least as the term is understood by his peers. The American Board of Pathology is considered the only reputable certifying organization for forensic pathology. Dr. Jones failed the board's exam in the 1980s. He still testifies in court that he's "board certified." But that's a reference to his membership in the American Academy of Forensic Examiners, which he has said publicly certified him without requiring him to take an exam.

Part of the problem is a lack of oversight. Elected county coroners and district attorneys shop out autopsies to private-practice medical examiners. The county pays doctors $550 for each autopsy, plus extra for other tests and services. Dr. Jones has dominated these referrals for years, a strong indication that coroners and district attorneys are happy with his work. And the state Supreme Court, although it tossed out his testimony in the Morris case, didn't stop him from testifying in other cases. Most experts agree that a medical examiner should be independent and find facts irrespective of their value to the prosecution.

Consider William Schifflett, convicted and sentenced to death in 2002 for the murder of his girlfriend's infant daughter. The indigent Schifflett asked the trial court for money to hire his own expert to review Dr. Jones's findings -- a crucial part of the state's case. He was denied. Schifflett's attorneys were able to get a former state medical examiner from a neighboring state to review Dr. Jones's autopsy for his appeal. Though the second autopsy raised real doubts about Schifflett's guilt, the state Supreme Court declined to even consider it, ruling that it was new evidence, and should have been introduced at trial.

That's not an uncommon ruling from an appellate court, but it illustrates just how important it is that state expert witnesses be reputable, credible, and accountable before ever stepping onto the witness stand.

Our state leaders should put an immediate end to Dr. Jones's autopsy operation. The state also needs to revisit every criminal case in which Dr. Jones has testified. Finally, we need to implement significant reforms as to how autopsies are conducted – we could start by requiring all contracted medical examiners to at least meet the profession's minimum standards. Until then, a cloud of suspicion hangs over every murder conviction that comes out of the state's courts.

DA Argues Infidelity, Money Motivated Killing

The Pelican Bay Star

December 7, 20XX-1
By Phillip Payne, State Court Correspondent

Pelican Bay -- Prosecutors are honing in on infidelity and money as reasons a former teacher might have killed her husband in 20XX-2.

Chris Alexander was shot six times in his living room, and his wife, Brandi, told police she believed he was killed after answering the front door.

Police recovered several .45 caliber shell casings in the foyer, outside the front door and in the flowerbed. But the only blood found in the house was under Chris Alexander in the living room.

Brandi Alexander also had traces of gunshot residue on her left hand. The defense plans to argue that it came from touching her husband's body.

The prosecution claims Brandi Alexander was angry about her husband's affair with another woman who spoke with him just minutes before he was killed.

That woman, Nikki Long, took the stand Wednesday afternoon and said she was on the phone with Chris Alexander for 30 minutes just moments before he was shot. Long said he had to hang up because his wife came in the room.

The district attorney told the jury that Brandi Alexander killed her husband for a $250,000 life insurance policy and because she found out he had at least two mistresses.

The former Public School teacher was arrested and charged in the slaying a week later.

Detective: Suspect Lied Night of Husband's Death

The Pelican Bay Star

December 9, 20XX-1
By Phillip Payne, State Court Correspondent

Pelican Bay -- Testimony in the second day of a former teacher's murder trial revealed that she lied to police on the night of her husband's slaying.

Officer Anece Baxter White told jurors Thursday that Brandi Alexander lied to her about a gun being in the couple's house. Only after she told her an empty gun holster was found under her bed did the Public School teacher say there was a .9-millimeter in the garage, Baxter White testified.

A friend of the victim, Chris Alexander, said in court that Alexander had owned a .45-caliber gun that is still missing -- the same type of gun used to kill Alexander.

An investigator testified he found no signs of forced entry or blood anywhere in the house except around the body of Chris Alexander. A neighbor who lives across the street also told the jury he heard gunshots the night of the killing, looked out and saw no one leave the Alexander house.

An aunt of Chris Alexander that went to the house the night of the crime testified that Brandi Alexander had gone into a bathroom to wash up. She later tested positive for gunshot residue on the back of her left hand.

Brandi Alexander was arrested and charged in the slaying a week after her husband's death.

Teacher's Attorney Blasts Investigation: Defense Claims Detective Left Details Out Of Report

The Pelican Bay Star

December 13, 20XX-2
By Phillip Payne, State Court Correspondent

Pelican Bay -- The defense for a former Public Schools teacher blasted police during her murder trial Monday, saying detectives did a sloppy and incomplete investigation.

Lead Detective Ed Morris spent most of the day on the stand telling jurors what Brandi Alexander told him about the night of her husband's death and defending his own report.

Defense attorney Ross Eastman ripped into Morris, claiming he'd left out details in his initial report that he included in his testimony -- facts such as inaccurate dates and who was at the crime scene the night of the slaying.

Morris told jurors he interviewed Brandi Alexander six days after the killing and that she had several inconsistencies in her story, mainly about the couple's security system. Alexander first said she heard the alarm go off while she was sleeping, then heard popping noises, Morris testified. But he said Alexander changed the story moments later, saying the popping sounds came first.

Brandi Alexander claims she found her husband shot on the living room floor and that someone else did it. She tested positive for gunshot residue, and there were no signs of forced entry or blood anywhere in the house except around the body.

Teacher's Murder Trial Resumes

The Pelican Bay Star

January 2, 20XX-1
By Phillip Payne, State Court Correspondent

Pelican Bay -- Testimony is expected to continue Thursday morning in the trial of a Public School teacher accused of killing her husband. Opening statements began Wednesday in the case.

The defense claims someone else shot Brandi Alexander' husband Chris as he answered their front door in June 20XX-2.

But the prosecution claims she killed her husband to collect a $250,000 life insurance policy. Prosecutors said Brandi Alexander was angry about her husband's affairs with two other women.

In court on Wednesday, one of those women claimed she spoke with Chris Alexander just minutes before he was killed.

Police recovered several .45 caliber shell casings in the house.

Brandi Alexander also had traces of gunshot residue on her left hand. The defense said that was because she touched her husband's body.

Juror Dismissed In Ex-Teacher's Murder Trial

The Pelican Bay Star

January 4, 20XX-1
By Phillip Payne, State Court Correspondent

Pelican Bay -- A juror was dismissed Friday in the murder trial of a former Public Schools teacher.

Brandi Alexander is accused of killing her husband, Chris Alexander, at their home.

Juror No. 5 was dismissed because she had been taking medication and was seen closing her eyes and not focusing on testimony Thursday.

The jury now has eight white members and four black members -- three of them women. Judge Jerry Parker noted a defense objection and moved forward.

Much of Friday's testimony focused on shell casings and bullet fragments in the house. Alexander was shot six times and died in his living room. Although the shell casings were found outside the front door, most of the bullet fragments were around and underneath the body.

The prosecution contended Brandi Alexander stood over her husband's body and shot him, sending bullets into the concrete underneath the living room carpet -- something a gun expert from the state crime lab said is possible.

Brandi Alexander claimed someone at their front door shot her husband while she was in the bedroom. She tested positive for traces of gunshot residue on the back of her left hand, investigators said.

The trial has ended for the weekend. Alexander could be sentenced to life in prison if she's found guilty.

Teacher Guilty!

The Pelican Bay Star

January 9, 20XX-1
By Phillip Payne, State Court Correspondent

It took a Calusa County Jury only two hours to reach a guilty verdict in Brandi Alexander's Alexander' murder trial.

"We the jury, find the defendant guilty as charged," read the court foreman.

Brandi Alexander showed no emotion Tuesday after she was found guilty of the 200XX-2 killing of her husband, Chris Alexander.

Chris Alexander' father said the verdict does little to numb his pain.

"I'm pleased with what the verdict was. I'm not happy, but pleased, because God confirmed what he showed me two and a half years ago," Chris Alexander Sr. said.

Chris Alexander was shot six times in the living room of the north Jackson home he shared with his wife in June 20XX-2. The gun has never been found.

During the trial, prosecutors alleged that Brandi Alexander killed her husband because he had two mistresses and also to cash in on a $250,000 life insurance policy.

Prosecutors also claimed gunshot residue found on her hand proved she fired the shots.

Defense attorneys called only one witness. The defense contended that Brandi Alexander was asleep in her bedroom when her husband was fatally shot and that she discovered his body after hearing popping noises.

"There's no direct evidence. There's not one piece of direct evidence you can seize or put your hands on and say 'I'm convinced beyond a reasonable doubt.' They build inference onto inference, and the law doesn't allow that," defense attorney Ross Eastman said.

After the verdict was read, Brandi Alexander' family members cried in the courtroom and did not want to speak as they left the courthouse.

Her attorneys said they will request a new trial.

Since the murder, Chris Alexander' family has continued a limited relationship with Brandi because of the couple's children.

Chris Alexander' father said he still questions why his son was murdered.

"When someone tells you point blank, 'I didn't have anything to do with your son's death,' and come to find out that person lied to you, that hurts. It really hurts." Mr. Alexander said.

Judge Jerry Parker sentenced Brandi Alexander to life in prison shortly after she was found guilty.

Retrial Set For Teacher Charged With Murder

The Pelican Bay Star
By Phillip Payne, State Court Correspondent

Pelican Bay -- A former public school teacher accused of killing her husband will be retried this week.

Brandi Alexander' retrial originally was scheduled for May, but attorneys for both sides said scheduling conflicts forced them to set a November date.

During her first trial, prosecutors claimed she killed Chris Alexander to cash in on a life insurance policy and because he had two mistresses.

Alexander was convicted in January and sentenced to life in prison, but that verdict was thrown out after Judge Jerry Parker ruled that prosecutors sought to keep blacks off the jury.

She was released on $150,000 bond.

The retrial starts Tuesday.

-Notes-

State of XXXXX
UNIFORM COMMITMENT TO CUSTODY
OF DEPARTMENT OF CORRECTIONS

THE CIRCUIT COURT OF CALUSA COUNTY, IN THE SPRING TERM of 20XX-8
IN THE CASE OF:

STATE OF XXXXXX

v.   CASE ID   : 20XX(-8)1492   DIVISION: D

DEFENDANT   :   Chris   Alexander
AKA(S)   :   Frostie

IN THE NAME AND BY AUTHORITY OF THE STATE OF XXXXX, TO THE SHERRIFF OF SAID COUNTY AND THE DEPARTMENT OF CORRECTIONS OF SAID STATE, GREETING:

THE ABOVE NAMED DEFENDANT HAVING BEEN DULY CHARGED WITH THE OFFENSE SPECIFIED HEREIN IN THE ABOVE STYLED COURT, AND HAVING BEEN DULY CONVICTED AND ADJUDICATED GUILTY OF AND SENTENCE FOR SAID OFFENSE BY SAID COURT, AS APPEARS FROM THE ATTACHED CERTIFIED COPIES OF INFORMATION FILED JUDGMENT AND SENTENCE, AND FELONY DISPOSITION AND SENTENCE DATA FROM WHICH ARE HEREBY MADE PARTS HEREOF;

NOW THEREFORE, THIS TO COMMAND YOU, THE SAID SHERIFF, TO TAKE AND KEEP, AND, WITHIN A REASONABLE TIME AFTER RECEIVING THIS COMMITMENT, SAFELY DELIVER THE SAID DEFENDANT, TOGETHER WITH ANY PERTINENT INVESTIGATION REPORT PREPARED IN THIS CASE, INTO THE CUSTODY OF THE DEPARTMENT OF CORRECTIONS OF THE STATE OF XXXXX: AND THIS IS TO COMMAND YOU, THE SAID DEPARTMENT OF CORRECTIONS, BY AND THROUGH YOUR SECRETARY, REGIONAL DIRECTORS, SUPERINTENDANTS, AND OTHER OFFICIALS, TO KEEP AND SAFELY IMPRISON THE SAID DEFENDANT FRO THE TERM OF SAID SENTENCE IN THE INSTITUTION IN THE STATE CORRECTIONAL SYSTEM TO WHICH YOU, THE SAID DEPARTMENT OF CORRECTIONS, MAY CAUSE THE SAID DEFENDANT TO BE CONVEYED OR THEREAFTER TRANSFERRED. AND THESE PRESENTS SHALL BE YOUR AUTHORITY FOR THE SAME. HEREIN NOT FAIL.

WITNESS THE HONORABLE JEREMY PARKER
JUDGE OF THE SAID COURT, AS ALSO CONNIE EVANS
CLERK, AND THE SEAL THEREOF, THIS
24th DAY OF May 20XX-8

BY: _Margaret Mills_

DEPUTY CLERK

IN THE FIRST JUDICIAL CIRCUIT IN AND FOR
CALUSA COUNTY, STATE OF XXXXX

CIRCUIT CRIMINAL DIVISON

STATE OF XXXXX   DIVISION: D
v.
<u>CHRIS ALEXANDER</u>   CASE NUMBER: 20XX(-8)1492
DEFENDANT

CERTIFICATE OF SERVICE

    I, Connie Evans, Clerk of the Circuit Court of the County of Calusa, State of XXXXX, having by law the custody of the seal and all records, books, documents and papers of or appertaining to the Circuit Court, do hereby certify that a true and correct copy of the Judgment and Sentence has been hand delivered to the State Attorney and mailed to the Defense Attorney.

    IN WITNESS WHEREOF, I have hereunto set my hand and seal of said Circuit Court, this 24th day of May A.D. 20XX-8.

CONNIE EVANS
As Clerk of Circuit Court

<u>Margaret Mills</u>

As Deputy Clerk
Circuit Criminal Division

IN THE CIRCUIT COURT, 1ST JUDICIAL
CIRCUIT
IN AND FOR CALUSA COUNTY, XXXXX
DIVISION   :   D
CASE NUMBER :   20XX(-8)1492

STATE OF XXXXX
v.
Chris Alexander
DEFENDANT

--JUDGMENT---

THE DEFENDANT, Chris Alexander, BEING PERSONALLY BEFORE
THIS COURT REPRESENTED WITH
PRIVATE ATTORNEY
Norm Pearson, Esquire
THE ATTORNEY OF RECORD AND THE STATE REPRESENTED BY ASSISTANT STATE
ATTORNEY
George Peabody Smalley, AND HAVING

Been tried and found guilty by a jury of the following crime(s): 1

COUNT	CRIME	STATUTE	COURT ACTION	DATE
1	Possession of a Controlled Substance, to wit, MARIJUANA	80112	GUILTY	16 April 20XX-8
2	Sale of a Controlled Substance, to wit, Marijuana	80112a	GUILTY	16 April 20XX-8

And no cause being shown why the defendant should not be adjudicated guilty, it is ordered that
the defendant is hereby adjudicated guilty of the above crime(s).

DEFENDANT Chris Alexander

                                      Division   : D
                                      Case Number : 20XX(-8)1492
                                      OBTS Number : 98421119

---SENTENCE---
THE DEFENDANT, BEING PERSONALLY BEFORE THIS COURT, ACCOMPANIED BY THE
DEFENDANT'S ATTORNEY OF RECORD, PRIVATE ATTORNEY Norm Pearson, Esquire
AND HAVING BEEN ADJUDGED GUILTY HEREIN, AND THE COURT HAVING BEEN GIVEN
THE DEFENDANT AN OPPORTUNITY TO BE HEARD AND TO OFFER MATTERS IN
MITIGATION OF SENTENCE, AND TO SHOW CAUSE WHY THE DEFENDANT SHOULD NOT
BE SENTENCED AS PROVIDED BY LAW AND NO CAUSE BEING SHOWN

IT IS THE SENTENCE OF THIS COURT THAT THE DEFENDANT:

Pay a fine of $2500.00, pursuant to appropriate XXXXX Statutes.

Is hereby committed to the custody of the Department of Corrections for a term of: 4 Years,
sentence to be suspended pending successful completion of 4 years probation.

---OTHER PROVISIONS---
AS TO COUNT(S) : 1
THE FOLLOWING MANDATORY/MINIMUM PROVISIONS APPLY TO THE SENTENCE
IMPOSED :

DEFENDANT Chris Alexander

                                      Division   : D
                                      Case Number : 20XX(-8)1492
                                      OBTS Number : 98421119
---OTHER PROVISIONS---
Sentencing guidelines filed.

IN THE EVENT THE ABOVE SENTENCE IS TO THE DEPARTMENT OF CORRECTIONS, THE
SHERIFF OF CALUSA COUNTY, XXXXX, IS HEREBY ORDERED AND DIRECTED TO
DELIVER THE DEFENDANT TO THE DEPARTMENT OF CORRECTIONS AT THE FACILITY
DESIGNATED BY THE DEPARTMENT TOGETHER WITH A COPY OF THIS JUDGMENT AND
SENTENCE AND ANY OTHER DOCUMENTS SPECIFIED BY XXXXX STATUTE
THE DEFENDANT IN OPEN COURT WAS ADVISED OF THE RIGHT TO APPEAL FROM THIS
SENTENCE BY FILING NOTICE OF APPEAL WITHIN 30 DAYS FROM THIS DATE WITH THE
CLERK OF THIS COURT AND THE DEFENDANT'S RIGHT TO THE ASSISTANCE OF
COUNSEL IN TAKING THE APPEAL AT THE EXPENSE OF THE STATE SHOWING OF
INDIGENCY.

DONE AND ORDERED IN CALUSA COUNTY, XXXXX, THIS 24TH DAY OF May 20XX-8

State of XXXXX
UNIFORM COMMITMENT TO CUSTODY
OF DEPARTMENT OF CORRECTIONS

THE CIRCUIT COURT OF CALUSA COUNTY, IN THE SPRING TERM of 20XX-8
IN THE CASE OF:

STATE OF XXXXX   CASE ID   : 20XX(-3)1898   DIVISION: D
v.
DEFENDANT   :   Nikki   Long
AKA(S)   :

IN THE NAME AND BY AUTHORITY OF THE STATE OF XXXXX, TO THE SHERIFF OF SAID
COUNTY AND THE DEPARTMENT OF CORRECTIONS OF SAID STATE, GREETING:

THE ABOVE NAMED DEFENDANT HAVING BEEN DULY CHARGED WITH THE
OFFENSE SPECIFIED HEREIN IN THE ABOVE STYLED COURT, AND HAVING BEEN DULY
CONVICTED AND ADJUDICATED GUILTY OF AND SENTENCE FOR SAID OFFENSE BY
SAID COURT, AS APPEARS FROM THE ATTACHED CERTIFIED COPIES OF INFORMATION
FILED JUDGMENT AND SENTENCE, AND FELONY DISPOSITION AND SENTENCE DATA
FROM WHICH ARE HEREBY MADE PARTS HEREOF;

NOW THEREFORE, THIS TO COMMAND YOU, THE SAID SHERIFF, TO TAKE AND
KEEP, AND, WITHIN A REASONABLE TIME AFTER RECEIVING THIS COMMITMENT,
SAFELY DELIVER THE SAID DEFENDANT, TOGETHER WITH ANY PERTINENT
INVESTIGATION REPORT PREPARED IN THIS CASE, INTO THE CUSTODY OF THE
DEPARTMENT OF CORRECTIONS OF THE STATE OF XXXXX: AND THIS IS TO COMMAND
YOU, THE SAID DEPARTMENT OF CORRECTIONS, BY AND THROUGH YOUR
SECRETARY, REGIONAL DIRECTORS, SUPERINTENDANTS, AND OTHER OFFICIALS, TO
KEEP AND SAFELY IMPRISON THE SAID DEFENDANT FRO THE TERM OF SAID
SENTENCE IN THE INSTITUTION IN THE STATE CORRECTIONAL SYSTEM TO WHICH
YOU, THE SAID DEPARTMENT OF CORRECTIONS, MAY CAUSE THE SAID DEFENDANT
TO BE CONVEYED OR THEREAFTER TRANSFERRED. AND THESE PRESENTS SHALL BE
YOUR AUTHORITY FOR THE SAME. HEREIN NOT FAIL.

WITNESS THE HONORABLE JEREMY PARKER
JUDGE OF THE SAID COURT, AS ALSO CONNIE EVANS
CLERK, AND THE SEAL THEREOF, THIS
21st DAY OF January 20XX-3

BY: Margaret Mills

DEPUTY CLERK

IN THE FIRST JUDICIAL CIRCUIT IN AND FOR
CALUSA COUNTY, STATE OF XXXXX

CIRCUIT CRIMINAL DIVISON

STATE OF XXXXX

V.

Nikki Long
DEFENDANT

DIVISION: D

CASE NUMBER: 20XX(-1)1898

CERTIFICATE OF SERVICE

I, Connie Evans, Clerk of the Circuit Court of the County of Calusa, State of XXXXX, having by law the custody of the seal and all records, books, documents and papers of or appertaining to the Circuit Court, do hereby certify that a true and correct copy of the Judgment and Sentence has been hand delivered to the State Attorney and mailed to the Defense Attorney.

IN WITNESS WHEREOF, I have hereunto set my hand and seal of said Circuit Court, this 21st day of January A.D. 20XX-3.

CONNIE EVANS
As Clerk of Circuit Court

Margaret Mills

As Deputy Clerk
Circuit Criminal Division

IN THE CIRCUIT COURT, 1ST JUDICIAL CIRCUIT
IN AND FOR CALUSA COUNTY, XXXXX
DIVISION   :   D
CASE NUMBER   :   20XX(-3)1898

STATE OF XXXXX
VS
Nikki Long
DEFENDANT

---JUDGMENT--

THE DEFENDANT, Nikki Long,   BEING PERSONALLY BEFORE
THIS COURT REPRESENTED WITH
PRIVATE ATTORNEY
Norm Pearson, Esquire
THE ATTORNEY OF RECORD AND THE STATE REPRESENTED BY ASSISTANT STATE
ATTORNEY
George Peabody Smalley, AND HAVING

Been tried and found guilty by a jury of the following crime(s): 1

COUNT	CRIME	STATUTE	COURT ACTION	DATE
1	Filing a false police report	80107	GUILTY	14 Dec 20XX-4

And no cause being shown why the defendant should not be adjudicated guilty, it is ordered that the defendant is hereby adjudicated guilty of the above crime(s).

DEFENDANT Nikki Long

Division   :   D
Case Number   :   20XX(-3)1898
OBTS Number   :   32323498

--SENTENCE--

THE DEFENDANT, BEING PERSONALLY BEFORE THIS COURT, ACCOMPANIED BY THE DEFENDANT'S ATTORNEY OF RECORD, PRIVATE ATTORNEY Norm Pearson, Esquire

AND HAVING BEEN ADJUDGED GUILTY HEREIN, AND THE COURT HAVING BEEN GIVEN THE DEFENDANT AN OPPORTUNITY TO BE HEARD AND TO OFFER MATTERS IN MITIGATION OF SENTENCE, AND TO SHOW CAUSE WHY THE DEFENDANT SHOULD NOT BE SENTENCED AS PROVIDED BY LAW AND NO CAUSE BEING SHOWN

IT IS THE SENTENCE OF THIS COURT THAT THE DEFENDANT:

Pay a fine of $750.00, pursuant to appropriate XXXXX Statutes. Is hereby committed to the custody of the Department of Corrections for a term of: 18 Months, sentence to be suspended pending successful completion of 2 years probation.

--OTHER PROVISIONS--
AS TO COUNT(S): 1
THE FOLLOWING MANDATORY/MINIMUM PROVISIONS APPLY TO THE SENTENCE IMPOSED:

None

DEFENDANT Nikki Long

Division   :   D
Case Number   :   20XX(-3)1898
OBTS Number   :   32323498

--OTHER PROVISIONS--
Sentencing guidelines filed.

IN THE EVENT THE ABOVE SENTENCE IS TO THE DEPARTMENT OF CORRECTIONS, THE SHERIFF OF CALUSA COUNTY, XXXXX, IS HEREBY ORDERED AND DIRECTED TO DELIVER THE DEFENDANT TO THE DEPARTMENT OF CORRECTIONS AT THE FACILITY DESIGNATED BY THE DEPARTMENT TOGETHER WITH A COPY OF THIS JUDGMENT AND SENTENCE AND ANY OTHER DOCUMENTS SPECIFIED BY XXXXX STATUTE

THE DEFENDANT IN OPEN COURT WAS ADVISED OF THE RIGHT TO APPEAL FROM THIS SENTENCE BY FILING NOTICE OF APPEAL WITHIN 30 DAYS FROM THIS DATE WITH THE CLERK OF THIS COURT AND THE DEFENDANT'S RIGHT TO THE ASSISTANCE OF COUNSEL IN TAKING THE APPEAL AT THE EXPENSE OF THE STATE SHOWING OF INDIGENCY.

DONE AND ORDERED IN CALUSA COUNTY, XXXXX, THIS 21st DAY OF January 20XX-3

State of XXXXX
UNIFORM COMMITMENT TO CUSTODY
OF DEPARTMENT OF CORRECTIONS

THE CIRCUIT COURT OF CALUSA COUNTY, IN THE SPRING TERM of 20XX-8
IN THE CASE OF:

STATE OF XXXXX   CASE ID   : 20XX(-6)1066   DIVISION: D
v.
DEFENDANT   : Nikki   Long
AKA(S)   :

IN THE NAME AND BY AUTHORITY OF THE STATE OF XXXXX, TO THE SHERRIFF OF SAID COUNTY AND THE DEPARTMENT OF CORRECTIONS OF SAID STATE, GREETING:

THE ABOVE NAMED DEFENDANT HAVING BEEN DULY CHARGED WITH THE OFFENSE SPECIFIED HEREIN IN THE ABOVE STYLED COURT, AND HAVING BEEN DULY CONVICTED AND ADJUDICATED GUILTY OF AND SENTENCE FOR SAID OFFENSE BY SAID COURT, AS APPEARS FROM THE ATTACHED CERTIFIED COPIES OF INFORMATION FILED JUDGMENT AND SENTENCE, AND FELONY DISPOSITION AND SENTENCE DATA FROM WHICH ARE HEREBY MADE PARTS HEROF;

NOW THEREFORE, THIS TO COMMAND YOU, THE SAID SHERIFF, TO TAKE AND KEEP, AND, WITHIN A REASONABLE TIME AFTER RECEIVING THIS COMMITMENT, SAFELY DELIVER THE SAID DEFENDANT, TOGETHER WITH ANY PERTINENT INVESTIGATION REPORT PREPARED IN THIS CASE, INTO THE CUSTODY OF THE DEPARTMENT OF CORRECTIONS OF THE STATE OF XXXXX: AND THIS IS TO COMMAND YOU, THE SAID DEPARTMENT OF CORRECTIONS, BY AND THROUGH YOUR SECRETARY, REGIONAL DIRECTORS, SUPERINTENDANTS, AND OTHER OFFICIALS, TO KEEP AND SAFELY IMPRISON THE SAID DEFENDANT FRO THE TERM OF SAID SENTENCE IN THE INSTITUTION IN THE STATE CORRECTIONAL SYSTEM TO WHICH YOU, THE SAID DEPARTMENT OF CORRECTIONS, MAY CAUSE THE SAID DEFENDANT TO BE CONVEYED OR THEREAFTER TRANSFERRED. AND THESE PRESENTS SHALL BE YOUR AUTHORITY FOR THE SAME. HEREIN NOT FAIL.

WITNESS THE HONORABLE JEREMY PARKER
JUDGE OF THE SAID COURT, AS ALSO CONNIE EVANS
CLERK, AND THE SEAL THEREOF, THIS
24th DAY OF February 20XX-6

BY: _Margaret Mills_

DEPUTY CLERK

IN THE FIRST JUDICIAL CIRCUIT IN AND FOR
CALUSA COUNTY, STATE OF XXXXX

CIRCUIT CRIMINAL DIVISON

STATE OF XXXXX   DIVISION: D
v.
Nikki Long   CASE NUMBER: 20XX(-6)1066
DEFENDANT

CERTIFICATE OF SERVICE

    I, Connie Evans, Clerk of the Circuit Court of the County of Calusa, State of XXXXX, having by law the custody of the seal and all records, books, documents and papers of or appertaining to the Circuit Court, do hereby certify that a true and correct copy of the Judgment and Sentence has been hand delivered to the State Attorney and mailed to the Defense Attorney.

    IN WITNESS WHEREOF, I have hereunto set my hand and seal of said Circuit Court, this 24th day of February A.D. 20XX-6.

CONNIE EVANS
As Clerk of Circuit Court

Margaret Mills

As Deputy Clerk
Circuit Criminal Division

IN THE CIRCUIT COURT, 1ST JUDICIAL CIRCUIT
IN AND FOR CALUSA COUNTY, XXXXX
DIVISION   : D
CASE NUMBER : 20XX(-6)1066

STATE OF XXXXX
VS
Nikki Long
DEFENDANT

---JUDGMENT--

THE DEFENDANT, Nikki Long,   BEING PERSONALLY BEFORE
THIS COURT REPRESENTED WITH
PRIVATE ATTORNEY
Norm Pearson, Esquire
THE ATTORNEY OF RECORD AND THE STATE REPRESENTED BY ASSISTANT STATE
ATTORNEY
George Peabody Smalley, AND HAVING

Been tried and found guilty by a jury of the following crime(s): 1

COUNT	CRIME	STATUTE	COURT ACTION	DATE
1	Possession of a Controlled Substance, to wit, MARIJUANA	80112	GUILTY	9 January 20XX-6

And no cause being shown why the defendant should not be adjudicated guilty, it is ordered that the defendant is hereby adjudicated guilty of the above crime(s).

DEFENDANT Nikki Long

Division   : D
Case Number   : 20XX(-6)1066
OBTS Number   : 32323498

--------------------------------------SENTENCE--

THE DEFENDANT, BEING PERSONALLY BEFORE THIS COURT, ACCOMPANIED BY THE DEFENDANT'S ATTORNEY OF RECORD, PRIVATE ATTORNEY Norm Pearson, Esquire

AND HAVING BEEN ADJUDGED GUILTY HEREIN, AND THE COURT HAVING BEEN GIVEN THE DEFENDANT AN OPPORTUNITY TO BE HEARD AND TO OFFER MATTERS IN MITIGATION OF SENTENCE, AND TO SHOW CAUSE WHY THE DEFENDANT SHOULD NOT BE SENTENCED AS PROVIDED BY LAW AND NO CAUSE BEING SHOWN

IT IS THE SENTENCE OF THIS COURT THAT THE DEFENDANT:

Pay a fine of $500.00, pursuant to appropriate XXXXX Statutes. Is hereby committed to the custody of the Department of Corrections for a term of: 1 Year, sentence to be suspended pending successful completion of 2 years probation.

--OTHER PROVISIONS--

AS TO COUNT(S) : 1

THE FOLLOWING MANDATORY/MINIMUM PROVISIONS APPLY TO THE SENTENCE IMPOSED :

None

DEFENDANT Nikki Long

Division   : D
Case Number   : 20XX(-6)1066
OBTS Number   : 32323498

--OTHER PROVISIONS--

Sentencing guidelines filed.

IN THE EVENT THE ABOVE SENTENCE IS TO THE DEPARTMENT OF CORRECTIONS, THE SHERIFF OF CALUSA COUNTY, XXXXX, IS HEREBY ORDERED AND DIRECTED TO DELIVER THE DEFENDANT TO THE DEPARTMENT OF CORRECTIONS AT THE FACILITY DESIGNATED BY THE DEPARTMENT TOGETHER WITH A COPY OF THIS JUDGMENT AND SENTENCE AND ANY OTHER DOCUMENTS SPECIFIED BY XXXXX STATUTE

THE DEFENDANT IN OPEN COURT WAS ADVISED OF THE RIGHT TO APPEAL FROM THIS SENTENCE BY FILING NOTICE OF APPEAL WITHIN 30 DAYS FROM THIS DATE WITH THE CLERK OF THIS COURT AND THE DEFENDANT'S RIGHT TO THE ASSISTANCE OF COUNSEL IN TAKING THE APPEAL AT THE EXPENSE OF THE STATE SHOWING OF INDIGENCY.

DONE AND ORDERED IN CALUSA COUNTY, XXXXX, THIS 24TH DAY OF February 20XX-6